HILLBILLY DRUG BABY
: THE STORY

T0159285

Book 2 of the Hillbilly Drug Baby series

ANDREA BRUNAIS

Virginia

Published in the United States by WriteLife Publishing
(an imprint of Boutique of Quality Books Publishing Company, Inc.)
www.writelife.com

978-1-60808-203-2 (p)
978-1-60808-204-9 (e)

Library of Congress Control Number: 2018957948

Book and Cover design by Robin Krauss, www.bookformatters.com

First editor: Pearlie Tan
Second editor: Olivia Swenson

Praise for
Hillbilly Drug Baby: The Story

"Andrea Brunais has won prestigious journalism and fiction prizes for a good reason: She represents the cream of the reporting/writing crop. *Hillbilly Drug Baby: The Story* emphasizes not only her (and her husband's) humanity, but also her professionalism. Andrea's prose is clear, crisp, descriptive, and often heartbreaking in this tale of a talented kid whose life was littered with broken promises and dreams before they met. A fine and revealing read."

—Dan Smith, author of *CLOG!* and
Virginia Communications Hall of Fame journalist

"Simply said, I could not stop reading *Hillbilly Drug Baby: The Story*. I was put through the wringer with its emotional real-life drama of hope and despair, tenderness and violence. The Quixote-like storyline will have any adult holding their breath as they cheer for the young man from Appalachia and the all-in effort of those trying to save him from his troubling past. I would challenge anyone not to become fiercely involved from page one."

—Mike Houtz, author of *Dark Spiral Down*

"Using her considerable journalistic skills, Andrea Brunais tells the brutal truth of what it's like to gamble on the toughest risk in the world of foster care—aged-out males. Honest, humane, frustrating, and patient, Andrea and Hal Gibson recount the details of what it is like to begin a pursuit of good intentions with a realistic expectation that it won't be easy. The first-person realization of the barriers of a stubborn will, learned helplessness, and the effects of poverty and ignorance is all soon realized, but that's just the beginning of the story. This is a compelling tale of a messy life and how it intersects with a couple who hope to bring reasoned order. The discovery of talent is a fortunate win but that alone is no promise of success. Not by a long shot. But read it for the beauty of the hope."

—Lisa Brock, author of *Goodbye College, Hello Life!*

Preface

As a journalist in Florida in the 1980s, I researched and reported on cocaine babies—babies who were born into the agonies of drug withdrawal. The technical name of the condition is "neonatal abstinence syndrome." Newborn drug babies go through drug withdrawal, played out in symptoms such as fever, vomiting, tremors, irritability, seizures, and inconsolable, high-pitched crying. They were said to be handicapped by severe physical and mental conditions from which they might not recover. So-called experts questioned their ability to learn in school or refrain from criminal acts in adulthood. The thinking went that their brains would never be quite right.

Meeting Jesse-Ray Lewis put a lie to much of that grim diagnosis (which experts are still arguing about today). Jesse-Ray was a drug baby, born addicted and destined to spend the first days of his life in distress. His mother indulged in a cornucopia of opiates and other drugs before, during, and after her pregnancy. Her problems were so immense that she walked off the job of mothering Jesse-Ray when he was six months old—or so his father and grandmother told him.

When he was nineteen, Jesse-Ray Lewis walked into my life. What I saw was Jesse-Ray's potential, which afforded me the opportunity to throw a life buoy to a lost, street-smart soul—a project that turned into something close to an obsession lasting five-and-a-half months. Far from being zombie-like and unable to control his impulses, Jesse-Ray was a fast talker with a quick mind and a strong desire to adopt a more tender demeanor. He turned out to be a freakishly talented writer whose raw output could be translated into hard-hitting verse—the poetry that makes up the first title in this series: *Hillbilly Drug Baby: The Poems*.

The tumult he brought into my life paled in comparison to the upheaval in my husband's, Hal Gibson, who neglected his own work to take Jesse-Ray under his wing. Hal's days would often start with a wake-up call to Jesse-Ray and end with listening to Jesse-Ray ruminate about his life. At least five days a week, Hal would drive Jesse-Ray to a Narcotics Anonymous meeting in the evening—a therapeutic group discussion for recovering drug users. When the meeting was over, Hal would pick him up, drive him home, and—if Jesse-Ray's mind was troubled—Hal would sit in the driveway with him for an extra hour or so as he spun out the details of his uncertainties about his future.

Both of us allowed him to enter our lives, and both of us believed that Jesse-Ray could rise above a past conditioned by crime, domestic violence, sorry foster-care experiences, homelessness, and drug use. Hal tried to move heaven and earth for Jesse-Ray, believing that if he could show Jesse-Ray one-on-one male guidance, care, and role-modeling, it would make all the difference.

Hillbilly Drug Baby: The Story is the chronicle of an Appalachian mountain-bred teen who waltzed into the life of two quixotic, altruistic, naive outsiders with grown children of their own. Hal and I had little to guide us but an all-embracing belief in the value of talent, the worth of hard work, the force of reason, and the transformative power of love.

How did those tenets guide us?

Jesse-Ray's talent was clear from the start in the way he'd give a quick-witted answer to a question or tell a story in down-to-earth Appalachian vernacular. Hal and I believed a combination of brains and hard work could put career goals within Jesse-Ray's reach. Further informing our mission was the belief that Hal would be able to help Jesse-Ray see that if he applied himself, he could escape a life that only promised poverty, jail, and other unsavory prospects.

Those were our values, dipped in the pragmatism we believed

would pry Jesse-Ray from his shaky perch at the edge of the criminal underworld. Amplifying everything was the love we had to offer—the love between elder and youth, between mentor and mentee—the kind of love that turns on lights, warms the soul, and makes miracles possible.

"No power can withstand divine Love," wrote Mary Baker Eddy in *Science and Health with Key to the Scriptures*, the Christian Science textbook to which I ascribe. She had many things to say about love, a word she catalogued as a synonym for God. The underpinnings of divine love bolstered my belief that what Hal and I had to offer was stronger than anything the world had ever presented to Jesse-Ray. I took comfort from another of Eddy's statements: "Love inspires, illumines, designates, and leads the way. Right motives give pinions to thought, and strength and freedom to speech and action." So inspired, once Hal and I had embarked on the course, neither of us could turn back easily.

Each chapter of this book begins with an excerpt from Jesse-Ray's poems. Each chapter ends with a brief, corresponding exploration of the issues raised in the hope of providing context and facts to inform a situation that we are still trying to make sense of.

Acknowledgments

Many people contribute to the success of a book. Publisher Terri Leidich came to the work with an understanding of youthful addicts and those who try to help them; without her compassion and encouragement, this story might have remained untold. Saundra Kelley always offered a clear-eyed vision of people and the manuscript; she had a way of tilting her head and fixing her gaze, staring into my soul and setting me straight. As a medical professional, mentor, and father, Mike Houtz offered on-point critiques at a key juncture. Laura McCarter read and offered critiques on more than one draft. Pearlie Tan put the same hard-nosed, unsentimental editing into *Hillbilly Drug Baby: The Story* as she did into the first book in the series, *Hillbilly Drug Baby: The Poems*, making both works immeasurably better.

During Jesse-Ray's journey through our lives, the folks at the Bluefield Union Mission extended helping hands and second chances, putting up with the need for sometimes uncomfortable confabs. They did their part, even when that meant going out on a limb, spending more money, making that extra phone call, or putting up with Jesse-Ray's BS for yet another hour or another day.

My husband, Hal Gibson, endured much psychological poking and probing (some of it unwelcome, I'm sure) as I interviewed and reinterviewed him for this book.

Jesse-Ray Lewis put himself out there, shared his vulnerabilities, accepted editing (and sometimes advice), and seemed to sincerely wish to employ his story to make the world a better place.

I thank them all.

Table of Contents

CHAPTER 1

Jesse-Ray Lewis walks out of the woods

> Curse this lost, broken life.
> I need someone
> But I push them away.
>
> Inside I'm screaming.
>
> Five million life tests and
> I've failed all of them.
>
> —Jesse-Ray Lewis, "Pain"

How to cast the story of Jesse-Ray Lewis, this man-child who walked into our lives as the Appalachian winter melted into spring? The story could take many turns. What would the headline be?

**Homeless Appalachian teen turns life around
with strangers' help**

**Boy who can't multiply becomes poetry phenomenon
at college**

Meth baby/crack baby beats odds, gets clean, writes book

**Barely literate meth-cook returns to the lure
of easy money**

Gang members execute tell-all poet in burst of gunfire

Any one of these scenarios seemed equally likely.

When we first met Jesse-Ray, my husband and I couldn't imagine how things would end. As time passed, the picture rarely become more comprehensible, and at the seeming close of the case, five and a half months after he came into our lives, the conclusion is only somewhat clearer.

The saga is over. Or was it a hopeless cause? A fool's errand? A story of thwarted redemption? At first, I saw a young man, by turns awkward and innocent, sometimes with a knowing smugness, at moments buckling under the weight of his crimes as a drug-dealer's enforcer, bedeviled by guilt. A motherless child with a brutish father, he was young and fresh enough that Hal and I took him as a stand-in for our own sons, who lived far from us and, unlike Jesse-Ray, had already broken our hearts. Later I saw that I'd been blinded by his promise. He came to us—an Appalachian poet with a guileless smile that was the envy of angels, but he left under circumstances that were nothing close to angelic.

Countless psychology and self-help books show how humans perpetuate the psychic traumas of our lives. We plunge back into familiar chaos so that we can keep trying to make the story end right, this time. Maybe *this* time, we can make it work. Children of alcoholics choose to marry alcoholics. An employee changes jobs repeatedly, moving from one impossible-to-please boss to the next. Because he feared divorce, one of my commitment-phobe friends refused to marry until he thought he found just the right woman whom he believed would never divorce him. In the end, she left.

I wondered what Hal and I were trying to make right. Hal and I had both been married before. We both had grown sons, and in both cases our relationships with those sons were strained. We also knew what it was like to have alcoholics and drug addicts at close range. We'd seen our own children grapple with the perils of alcoholism and addiction in their teen years. Perhaps we longed to be über-parents at this late stage in life. Maybe we thought Jesse-Ray would soak up the antidrug messages more than our own children had, because for him, those messages were novel. He'd never heard them at home. And he'd certainly never heard them from a compassionate couple who offered the stability lacking in his own upbringing.

I think my role also held a slightly more exploitive note than Hal's—that of a talent scout. I suspected that Jesse-Ray's heartrending experiences combined with his ability to write could propel him to literary stardom in a world newly appreciative of all things Appalachian, not to mention a world newly awake to opioid addiction. The current crop of bestselling books (*Hillbilly Elegy*), star-studded movies ("The Glass Castle"), and Oscar-nominated documentaries ("Heroin(e)") suggested that the story of Jesse-Ray's life was a train wreck full of potentially bestselling elements. As soon as I discovered that Jesse-Ray had an aptitude for writing, I shepherded him into creating a chapbook of poetry with me as his mentor.

Hal's motivation was purer. Raised in a trusting, sheltered environment in the US Panama Canal Zone, he was often free to roam the jungles during his childhood, where the shamans taught him to catch big lizards for dinner and identify vines from which to drink pure water. To him, home represented safety and community, with the tree canopies and the sea providing daily escapes into nature. So it came as a shock to Hal when his parents decided he was old enough to leave home at seventeen, shipping him away to live with his maternal grandparents in Miami. He had been raised with the law of the jungle—the *real* jungle—but his upbringing didn't prepare him for life in the big city, and he felt cast adrift and very alone. Now he was positioned to spare Jesse-Ray the same grievous feelings of isolation.

During Hal's formative years, he also nurtured animals, including a mouse and a tarantula. Friends and neighbors would bring him creatures needing care, such as birds that had fallen from their nests, and he fed them round the clock, successfully saving many of them. Jesse-Ray was a perfect candidate to trigger Hal's rescue instincts. At nineteen, Jesse-Ray's character was still emerging, and he was trying to reject his past, which included drugs and crime. His problems seemed solvable. Dirty clothes could be washed. A higher education could be acquired. Spiritual horizons could be broadened.

Hal and I each have two children from our previous marriages— four grown children between us. Likewise, we each come from families of six children. I would have loved to have had more children of my own. Not Hal. He wasn't even wild about the idea of having two. To him, babies represented nothing but duties and chores. And yet, with our own children grown and far away, Hal was a willing partner in opening our lives to this new obligation. Jesse-Ray had received so little of the good things in life—so little good parenting, so few role models—that we convinced ourselves of the power of our influence. We saw promise, and we thought our belief in him would be enough to vanquish even his own doubts.

Hal was the first to encounter Jesse-Ray when a representative of the Bluefield Union Mission ushered the teenager into our safe house. The "safe house" was really just the lower story of the house next door to where Hal and I lived. It was about the size of a hotel's extended-stay suite, but we employed the term as a way to recognize the purpose we had assigned to the structure. Hal showed the staff member and Jesse-Ray how to unlock the door using the keypad lock, which operated by punching in a code rather than using a key.

Hal didn't get to spend more than a couple of minutes with Jesse-Ray, but he glimpsed the impression of an agreeable young man. Jesse-Ray's status as an aged-out foster child also caught his attention. Through my communications job at Virginia Tech, Hal and I had met several aged-out foster children, a class of young people whose state support abruptly ends when they reach their late teens or early twenties. Upon aging out of foster care, many of them couch-surfed, aimless. Some of them needed just a little encouragement, a little money, and a little guidance to get back into school. After meeting them at a university-sponsored panel to inform the community about their plight, I'd talked to Hal about the possibility of us helping out such children a few years down the road when we retired.

My interest in doing volunteer work in this field came from my background as a journalist, when I had researched and written newspaper editorials about public policies that cried out for change. Through the mid-1990s in Florida, the child protection laws elevated "family reunification" over the welfare of the child, resulting in children being placed back into dangerous homes, where many were further abused or killed. Only when children's advocates and journalists like me continued to make a stink was the law reformed.

While Hal and I were too old to take in young foster children and raise them to adulthood, I believed we could help an older teen on the road to independence without much inconvenience to ourselves. Such a project would satisfy my altruistic instincts without turning our lives upside down. Knowing my interest, Hal couldn't wait to tell me about our new tenant.

After we bought the ramshackle residence next door, which had rotting ceilings and walls, obsolete plumbing, and faulty electrical work, Hal employed his skills as a builder and craftsman for more than a year to cleverly redesign the house to create two units. When the upper unit was eventually completed, we planned to rent out the rooms to supplement our income. He had just completed renovations on the lower story when Jesse-Ray walked into our lives.

We had decided to commit the finished portion to the nearby Bluefield Union Mission, a local charity less than a mile from our home that provided lodging to people in need. We were volunteers and supporters of the mission's, having helped with Christmas and Thanksgiving meal preparations during the decade we'd lived in Bluefield.

We had also become friends with the executive director of the Bluefield Union Mission, Craig Hammond. Craig also ran the News and Brew, a downtown coffee shop since closed, and at the time, he was also attempting to build up a news website. We had in common an interest in news and in politics, and I would regularly stop by the News and Brew for a chat and to learn more about my adopted city. Craig was a font of knowledge, having served a term as Bluefield's mayor.

We had always found Craig to be refreshingly open-minded. We had batted about ideas for different ways to reinvigorate the town, such as attracting tourists by making Bluefield a hub for the region's railroad history. Craig would always get excited about possibilities, no matter the topic. When we broached the idea of turning the lower story of the house next door into a safe house for the mission to use, Craig was enthusiastic.

Typically, the Bluefield Union Mission puts people up at motels that are—shall we say—not luxe. When people need a temporary roof over their heads, the mission pays for short-term lodging, usually about three days' worth. Our safe house, completed in early 2017, would fulfill a need for slightly more upscale lodging, which could accommodate traveling missionaries, youth groups on summer service trips, people whose homes had burned down, or interstate travelers with engine trouble, for example. We charged the mission rent to cover taxes, insurance, utilities, and other expenses, but little more. The safe house was not designed to be a money-making proposition.

Craig signed a simple rental contract with us, and the choice of tenants was up to him. Hal provided the Bluefield Union Mission staff with their own unique keypad code, because they never knew what hour of the night or day someone might turn up needing a bed. Although we lived next door, we were not expected to have contact. Hal would be called in only to clean the premises between lodgers.

But instead of traveling missionaries or a family with car trouble, our first lodger was Jesse-Ray Lewis, a former cocaine-and-meth baby. This homeless boy-man had walked out of the woods, out from under the tree he'd been sleeping beneath, in search of a new life. What did he want?

When I contemplate what made Jesse-Ray tick or where his life might go, my mind takes me back to the shimmer and shine of the morning we met, an emotionally searing moment that seems sharper and more poignant with time. I met Jesse-Ray on Saturday, the day following his first night at the safe house. I usually came home weekends as I worked in Blacksburg, Virginia, about an hour away, where I kept a small studio apartment during the week.

We knew almost nothing about him; the staff at the Bluefield Union Mission had told Hal few details. At that point, they knew only that Jesse-Ray had been in foster care and now was seemingly without resources. We also knew nothing about teen homelessness, which is more common than most people think. I hadn't expected anyone homeless to be so young.

After we had our morning coffee, Hal went next door to check on things. Under our original plan, Hal would not have stepped foot on the property, preferring that his identity as landlord was not known to anyone staying there. But because Jesse-Ray was an aged-out foster child, Hal had disclosed his landlord status to Jesse-Ray, and he couldn't resist knocking on the door to check on Jesse-Ray's needs. When he returned, he said that he'd spotted only junk food in the safe house kitchen, the typical white-bread-and-sugar products that get donated to charities like the Bluefield Union Mission and are handed out to those who might otherwise go hungry.

I quickly whipped up an omelet to bring over to Jesse-Ray. Though I agreed with keeping our distance from the Bluefield Union Mission's lodgers, I went next door with Hal. We did not wish for the operation of a safe house to complicate our lives. We were to be landlords only. We were not anyone's keeper. The mission's staff was supposed to check the lodgers in, keep them supplied with food and toiletries if necessary, and let us know when they had checked out. Our role was to be limited. We were not ready to take on an aged-out foster child of our own.

Or so we thought. Clearly, something about Jesse-Ray had already touched Hal.

I remember the moment I saw Jesse-Ray as clear as day.

He had light skin, light brown hair, brown eyes, and pants that scraped the floor. The epithet "big galoot" sprang to mind. He was bigger than Hal, and Hal wore extra-large sizes and shopped in big-and-tall specialty stores. Jesse-Ray's manner was reticent, hesitant. He seemed a little shy.

He swallowed the eggs as if he hadn't eaten for days as he stood at the breakfast bar that Hal had built. Confusion permeated his expression, but he attempted to be personable. He looked us in the eyes as we conversed politely. He flashed a smile of even white teeth. His round face made him seem almost cherubic. He was a good-looking galoot.

Once he downed his food, he shuffled over to the kitchen counter to where his grimy fabric Bob Marley bag lay. It held what I later learned were pretty much his sole possessions: swim trunks that doubled as underwear, a pack of wet wipes, a gold ring, two cotton kerchiefs he called "gang flags," a crumpled grocery-store bag that constituted a wallet for his driver's license and his drug-smoking pipe. That was all.

He told us a little about himself. He had been sleeping outside, under a tree, and then he had moved inside a crumbling, abandoned house. He had been homeless for weeks, maybe months. He had survived without heat during the winter, through freezing temperatures and occasional snow. It was February, and the blustery days were only just ending.

He told us that he had been a foster child. He had worked in a coal mine. He had a father who was not currently in the picture. Jesse-Ray had also been involved with selling drugs, but he said he had turned his back on that life. He had walked into the Bluefield Union Mission looking for food, shelter, and help.

Physically, he reminded me of the young men on my mother's side of the family—large, shuffling Midwestern farm boys with a laid-back manner, a good heart, and an eye for a story. Hal and Jesse-Ray were both big guys, more than six feet tall, and it wasn't such a stretch to imagine that Jesse-Ray could be Hal's grandson.

Standing in the kitchen of the safe house, Hal and I locked eyes, making an instant decision about this person who was now our tenant, even though we knew little about him other than that he had no home, no family to turn to, and no belongings bigger than a box of tissues.

"You can stay here," I said. "Assuming that the Bluefield Union Mission agrees, that is. We'll ask them to let you live here until you can get your life in order. Hal and I have just three rules."

Typically, Hal and I would have talked before announcing such a big decision. But I had read agreement in Hal's eyes. Even if we had stopped to confer, I doubt we would have changed course. Without giving much consideration to how complicated things might get, we were already on our path. Fortunately, I had the presence of mind to set minimal rules at the outset. I knew the odds were good that Craig would agree to allow Jesse-Ray to stay longer than the usual three days. I also suspected, rightly, that no one at the Bluefield Union Mission would have time to craft or enforce rules, even though taking on a young person with a questionable background and history of drug use would seem to be a situation that cried out for rules. That job would be left to us. Hal looked on approvingly.

"No alcohol or drugs," I stated. "You have to work. And you have to go to school."

Relief hit Jesse-Ray's face, but his next words stunned me. "This is the first time in ten years I haven't had to worry about the roof over my head."

I drew a deep breath. How could a child be expected to worry about where he would sleep? It didn't occur to me that we might not know exactly how much truth there was to Jesse-Ray's pronouncements. But at that moment, I believed him 100 percent. I felt sad and shocked and sorry for Jesse-Ray.

Weeks later, we learned that he had been high on meth and marijuana at this first meeting.

"I remember talking to a lady with flames shooting out of her head," he said with a lopsided grin when I asked him what he remembered about our first conversation. There was no mystery where that visual came from—at the time my hair was dyed a vibrant auburn. "And the lady had a polka-dotted snake crawling around her neck," he added. I had worn a dotted scarf.

"Do you remember anything that we said?" I asked.

"Not really."

"What did you do after we left?"

"I just went back to sleep."

Unaware of this, I went back to my job, and Hal secured permission from Craig for Jesse-Ray to stay in the safe house indefinitely. For the Bluefield Union Mission, working with an aged-out foster child was an experimental commitment, one that Craig was willing to undertake. With the same speed he had agreed to the safe-house idea, he assented to extending the normal length of stay for this aged-out foster child. Craig said he would welcome Jesse-Ray as a volunteer, but he did not demand work as repayment for room and board. However, Hal and I insisted that Jesse-Ray walk down to the Bluefield Union Mission for daily work shifts. We knew enough about recovering addicts to realize that structure was vital. Leaving him with too much time on his hands would invite trouble. And the mission always needed extra hands, as they served lunch seven days a week, helped people with overdue bills and emergency needs, and operated a thrift store that saw constant traffic from shoppers and people dropping off donations.

Jesse-Ray developed a routine during the first few days. He showed up at the mission six days a week to work and pick up food. In the early days, most of his waking hours were spent there. While Jesse-Ray was doing his volunteer shift, Hal was able to attend to his own labors for a few hours, which consisted of completing renovations to the top half of the residence where Jesse-Ray lived.

But after hours, Hal began staying up well past midnight, scouring the Internet for information so that he could better understand the needs of a recovering addict, including uncovering resources such as the nightly Narcotics Anonymous meeting in downtown Bluefield. Exploratory calls were made to see whether Jesse-Ray might be eligible for government social services such as food stamps or educational grants. Soon Hal was spending hours every day making phone calls and driving Jesse-Ray to government offices to make applications.

Before Jesse-Ray's arrival, Hal's day-to-day work involved constructing things with wood or plastic pipe or metal. As he renovated the upstairs of the safe house, he worked with his hands. But, presented with the opportunity, he didn't shy away from a flesh-and-blood project. He devoted hours each day to helping Jesse-Ray forge a new body, mind, and spirit.

Hal and I talked on the phone morning and night during the work week, sharing news about our days. After Jesse-Ray's arrival, he was often the central subject of our conversations.

Soon after Jesse-Ray had arrived, he had shown Hal his gang flags and said that he wanted to repeat the demonstration for me. In Jesse-Ray's mind, we needed to understand his attachment to the flags, as if understanding this would somehow engender key insights about him. It was significant that he wanted to show me his gang flags, because at least one of the flags was always supposed to be kept hidden from the view of any outsider. He had quickly welcomed Hal into his inner circle, but I wasn't around during the week, so he and I had not yet bonded. During this show-and-tell about his gang flags, I got a taste of how deeply the gang world still had hooks in him. Despite his having taken up residence next door to our home, his mind was elsewhere, constantly pondering his action-packed past.

It was a Sunday, about a month into our relationship and the first time we'd allowed him inside our home. The three of us were sitting and talking in the living room, which adjoins the dining room. I went into the kitchen to make tea. As I clinked spoons and cups, Jesse-Ray walked over to the dining room table and began to spread out his squares of fabric.

Hal hissed at me from the doorway, signaling for me to pay attention because the gang-flag display was solemn business for Jesse-Ray. Jesse-Ray's moods mattered to Hal, who was still in the early days of his infatuation with the idea that he could lead Jesse-Ray to embrace a new path. Jesse-Ray had already said things about his past that I regarded skeptically, but Hal was always accepting of everything Jesse-Ray said. He gave Jesse-Ray's opinions more weight than I did. Most of the time, I didn't blame Hal. Jesse-Ray's vulnerability during this initial period of early recovery caused Hal's nurturing instincts to kick in. The first days when an addict meets the world without the protective haze of drugs or alcohol can be a time of ragged emotions and tumbling thoughts. Hal was filled with empathy. He was still the little boy who cared for injured birds.

But this was over the top. I looked back at Hal, eyes wide. I couldn't believe that Hal would grant what I considered to be outsized respect to the cockeyed view that pieces of cloth—no matter what you called them—were objects requiring ceremonious attention.

I glanced over from the kitchen sink and saw Jesse-Ray carefully caressing what looked like two scraps of fabric. Clearly he was not yet ready to stick them in a drawer, give them away, burn them or consign them to a trash heap.

I joined him at the dining room table.

He launched into a lengthy explanation. The flags were symbols of his gang, whose members he had psychologically fused with, fought alongside, and probably committed felonies with.

Those men (or were they boys, like him?) still had a hold on him. Their ties had been closer than blood. Their voices inhabited his mind, even as he stood at the altar of our dining room table to demonstrate the proper way to fold the flags.

Jesse-Ray ran his fingers along a crease.

"You can never let your flag touch the ground," he explained.

He showed me the black one first. He explained that it could be used to wipe off a knife or a gun or to mop something up, even blood. Maybe especially blood. The folding was painstakingly slow as Jesse-Ray's hands shook slightly, either from drug use or drug withdrawal.

He began by marking the center of the kerchief.

I shifted, impatient with the pace. Hal gave me a look, signaling that as foolish-seeming as the ritual was, the folding was a significant act for Jesse-Ray.

I found myself holding back laughter after spotting the words "100 percent cotton" and "Made in China" on the selvage. The kerchief reminded me of one I had bought at Walmart a few years back that was adorned with peace signs. Like Jesse-Ray's, my kerchief also said "100 percent cotton" and "Made in China." Despite its lavish drug profits, clearly Jesse-Ray's gang was more accustomed to discount stores than high-end boutiques. I don't know why this surprised me. I guess I expected a high-level street gang to order its uniforms and accessories from a specialized supplier, as do the judiciary and baseball teams.

Jesse-Ray explained that the first fold meant family, the second fold meant community, and the third fold meant that each gang member would take a bullet on the other's behalf. His gang members would always have his back. I wondered what he might say if I told him that when I wear my pink-and-purple "peace" kerchief tied around my neck, I sometimes think that the almighty love-force of the universe has my back.

Clearly, we came from different worlds. Jesse-Ray did not see what I saw: a piece of red cotton cloth with white paisley print. To me, it wasn't talismanic; it didn't represent blood oaths or secret societies. In contrast, he ascribed magic to the threads, infusing them with a significance they did not possess outside the codes of gangs. As he showed me how he tucked each flag was into his back pocket—one concealed, the other revealed—I wondered how long it would take before he realized that these scraps of fabric had no actual power. I wondered when he would give them up.

Soon, I thought. Hal would talk him out of his belief in the power of gang flags. I was almost sure of it. Reason would prevail.

But the demonstration wasn't over. The tone and tenor of Jesse-Ray's mood shifted slightly as he moved on to the folding of the red flag. During this part of the show-and-tell, he adopted an even graver mien. The red flag was his passport to his netherworld. He explained that the red kerchief was never to be used for any practical purpose—not to mop up blood or clean a knife or carry out any other item on the gang's to-do list. To Jesse-Ray, the red flag was his identifier, a talisman he was forbidden to display to anyone but another gang member.

I chose to see his words and actions through a positive lens. I believed the fact that Jesse-Ray allowed us to view the sacrosanct red gang flag showed that on some level, a bond was established that would prompt Jesse-Ray to recognize at least some of our viewpoints. Even if only slightly, the world looked different to him after spending a little time with us. At least he trusted us enough to share the significance of his flags.

For the first three or four weeks, Hal allowed Jesse-Ray to tuck his gang flags into his pocket before he left the safe house as long as neither the red nor the black was visible. Only later did Hal insist that he leave them behind when they would go on errands.

During those first weeks, Jesse-Ray started to recognize what sober living felt like and how a society of rules functioned. It seemed like we were moving forward, though I wanted to hear more from Jesse-Ray about what had motivated him to seek help from the Bluefield Union Mission in the first place.

"I was tired of being high and not giving a shit," he explained, under my persistent questioning. Later I wondered if that motivator—little more than a fleeting discomfort, perhaps—would be enough to spark lasting change. But as we got to know him initially, I took him at his word.

As the days and weeks passed, Hal and I realized with some joy that we had started putting spokes on the wheel of his new life.

Six days a week, Jesse-Ray showed up for his volunteer shifts at the Bluefield Union Mission, which was a short walk from the safe house. Every evening, Hal took him to Narcotics Anonymous meetings. Jesse-Ray could have walked to the meetings, but Hal wanted to spare him the risks associated with the seedy stretch of Bluefield Avenue that ran between our house and downtown. If a drug dealer approached him, the temptation might be too strong.

Jesse-Ray was also expected to keep the safe house tidy as part of his daily routine. In addition, Hal investigated social services as well as college aid and saw to it that Jesse-Ray was conditionally enrolled at the community college.

Then we reached the ninety-day mark—a milestone in the twelve-step meeting world where "ninety meetings in ninety days" is a prized goal. We took him out for Mexican food to celebrate. Jesse-Ray Lewis—as far as we knew—was clean and sober.

I had other reasons to celebrate. My interest in Jesse-Ray was tinged with the thrill of discovery when I realized he had the heart of a poet. He wrote verse with rap rhythms and a willingness to expose his soul.

To encourage his writing habit, I bought him a secondhand computer. Hal hooked the computer up to the Internet so Jesse-Ray could send me his first-draft poems, which frequently featured odd rhyme schemes. Jesse-Ray began to write late at night, composing lines as he listened to a hard-driving beat. His verse most often reflected dark thoughts about a violent past. His output consisted of short rhymed lines and amped-up verbs that weren't so much thought up as they were spat out. As for subject matter, his creations bored into disturbing subjects. Some read like ransom notes from Hell.

Jesse-Ray often said that, without the outlet of his writing, he didn't think he would have stayed sane or even alive. Each new draft of a poem showed me that Jesse-Ray had a riveting story to tell, one that I believed could take off during this national moment of interest in Appalachia illustrated by books such as *Hillbilly Elegy* and the numbing cascade of news stories on red-state voters following the US presidential election in 2016—not to mention worldwide news coverage of Appalachia's high numbers of drug overdose deaths.

Along the way, he seemingly began to commit to his own survival, albeit in a halting and halfway fashion. He wrote, and I helped block his words into stanzas and lines. Between his writing and my editing, we began to stitch together a chapbook of verse.

Hal and I offered mentorship, the government gave food stamps, and the Bluefield Union Mission paid for his shelter. Jesse-Ray's fellow workers at the mission shared feedback, camaraderie, and advice. People who ran nonprofits in the Bluefield area talked to him about his health and walked him through the application process for college tuition assistance. If it takes a village to raise a child, it seemed the village elders were in place.

How would Jesse-Ray accept the help of strangers? The people at the charity? My husband? Me? We didn't know. Perhaps we should have looked harder, and sooner, for clues.

At the same time, however, we felt nothing but hope for this motherless child on the cusp of adulthood.

Do incurable "drug babies" exist?

The crack epidemic of the 1980s sparked a wave of stories about cocaine babies. According to Kali Holloway of the AlterNet news service, commentators whipped up "widespread fearmongering directed toward cocaine-addicted mothers and their children." Small heads, irritability, and poor muscle tone were the marks of crack babies. Overheated rhetoric branded the newborns mentally deficient and destined to commit crimes.

During that era, a prominent Washington Post columnist suggested rounding up drug-using pregnant women and confining them to boot camps, placing them under house arrest, or incarcerating them in a practical, secure location to halt the onset of a bio-underclass. He defined this underclass as "a generation of physically damaged cocaine babies whose biological inferiority was stamped at birth."

Feminists and others decried the movement to stigmatize and jail women who used drugs or alcohol. "Melodramatic crack-mother stories shrouded all discussion of substance abuse in pregnancy with the aura of criminality," writes Janet Lynn Golden, a history professor and author of the 2005 book, *Message in a Bottle: The Making of Fetal Alcohol Syndrome.*

Crack babies were mostly associated with the black community, involving waves of births in big cities such as Philadelphia and Washington, DC. In contrast, today's opioid-addiction crisis devastates white communities, many in Appalachia. Many of the same people who objected to the fearmongering of the 1980s now question the double standard. They see a softening of the rhetoric that once demonized drug-abusing mothers, now that many of those mothers are white.

Here are the stats: Almost one-quarter of Medicaid recipients who are pregnant filled a prescription for an opioid pain reliever in 2007. That percentage is significant and alarming, as any opioid use is linked to addiction, even when the drugs are legally prescribed. In turn, doctors have tied this wave of prescription drug use to the rising numbers of babies exposed to powerfully addictive drugs in utero.

Adding to the evidence, Tennessee experienced a fifteen-fold increase in drug-addicted babies born over ten years during the decade leading up to 2013, which so alarmed state policymakers that they instructed all Tennessee health departments to report the births of such babies to ensure complete data. Rates are highest in the eastern, Appalachian portion of the state. Tennessee's startling rise is echoed in a study in Florida hospitals finding a tenfold increase in babies born addicted over a sixteen-year period starting in 1995. A later study, which analyzed data of newborns suffering withdrawal-type symptoms in six Florida hospitals, found that 99.6 percent of the babies had been exposed to opioids in utero, "highlighting the issue of opioid use in women of childbearing age."

Politics of race and sex aside, what, medically speaking, can be concluded about babies who exhibit symptoms of drug withdrawal when they are born?

Predictions of a generation of crack babies damaged for life turned out to have been overblown. However, alcohol's damaging effects on fetuses has proved to be of lasting import, even though doctors initially resisted the fact that alcohol might be dangerous.

What about today's drug babies? An addicted baby (one who suffers from drug-withdrawal symptoms such as fever and vomiting as well as irritability and constant crying) is born about every twenty-five minutes. Most babies stay for about three weeks in the hospital, racking up bills of almost $100,000 per infant, with Medicaid picking up most of the tab.

At a Centers for Disease Control and Prevention conference in April 2017, researchers presented data linking drug-addicted babies with early childhood disabilities such as developmental delays and language impairment. A study of more than 2,000 drug-addicted babies born between 2000 and 2006 showed that the children's performance in reading and math test scores in the third, fifth, and seventh grades grew progressively worse. The authors found that addiction at birth "is strongly associated with poor and deteriorating school performance."

However, according to the Centers for Disease Control and Prevention, "Data on long-term developmental outcomes are limited." Doctors aren't yet prepared to say whether the damage visited on babies like Jesse-Ray Lewis is long lasting and irreversible.

CHAPTER 2

Details of Jesse-Ray's life emerge

I cry inside.
I ask why
disaster strikes.

I get in a fight
not physical—
but a mental war.
Defeated
like a statistic on a board.

—Jesse-Ray Lewis, "Mental War"

Jesse-Ray's gravitation to gang life sprang from a drug-infested childhood in rural Appalachia with an absent mother, a father who was indifferent at best and violent at worst, and a school system that failed to properly support a young boy who often showed up in a drug haze. As Jesse-Ray told me more about his past, I knew we had a story. Doubts set in, however, on how best to tell it. Only one thing was certain. As we drew the details out of him, we needed to be wary of the devils we woke.

During the week while I was at my job, Hal would devote hours to Jesse-Ray. Hal had all but given up his own work, which was becoming an issue because every lost day took money out of our pockets. Our home needed to be insulated and, because it was originally constructed from brick, the job required gutting the old plaster and building new interior walls to be covered with sheetrock. The process was elaborate but it was the only way to create the space for insulation we needed. Meanwhile, for every year that passed without insulation, we were forced to pay hundreds of dollars extra in electric bills during the snowy mountain winters, even when we cut off the heat to half the rooms. Our home also needed repairs to a kitchen last updated in 1950, but before that, he needed to complete renovations to the upstairs half of the safe house so it could be rented out.

Hal was already behind schedule, in part because of his big heart. He would drop everything to go to a friend's aid. One caller was his good friend Lawrence Calfee, a carpenter. Hal had been a master Jaguar technician for more than a dozen years in Oregon, Texas, and Florida, and his knowledge of cars is voluminous. Hal had cautioned Lawrence not to toss his keys up on the dash of his Ford E-350 heavy-duty van.

"Sooner or later, you're going to lose them down the slot and into the defroster vent," Hal warned. "And when you do that, the only way to retrieve them is to take out the whole dash. You'll be paying the dealer by the hour for an eight-hour job."

Lawrence didn't listen. One day Lawrence was at the home of a customer in Paintlick, Virginia, ready to begin his day's work, when he tossed his keys on the dash as usual. Because the van's vent design is a slot, not a grill, the keys slid and disappeared as Hal had predicted.

"The keys went right down that slot and into the defroster," Hal explained to me later. "That's the vent up by the windshield. You can't see anything, and you can't get to it, because the windshield and the dash come together at that spot, so you can't get anything down there to fish the keys out."

A sheepish Lawrence called Hal, who jumped in his Jeep for the forty-five-minute drive to Paintlick to bail out his friend. But Hal lacked the specialized tools to remove everything that had to be taken out before extracting the dash: the AC blower motor housing, the center console bolted over the engine, the steering wheel column, assorted switches, and the radio. He had brought a hole saw, and Lawrence agreed to a shortcut that would damage the van's dash but get the job done. The job would still be complex, but sawing would be quicker than completely removing the dash. Hal bored holes at either end of the vents and—four hours later—Lawrence's keys were back in his hand, along with a collection of pens and coins that had also accumulated in the defroster.

Lawrence was grateful to Hal for sparing him the prospect of towing his van to the dealership and paying several hundred dollars to get his keys back. Equally important, the relationship wasn't one-sided. Over the years, Lawrence came to Hal's aid many times as well. Still, Hal was prone to put other's needs first and could be easily sidetracked.

He hadn't expected the Jesse-Ray project to be so labor intensive, so he was surprised that much of his day was spent making arrangements for social services, chauffeuring, anticipating needs, and making sure Jesse-Ray was punctual for his appointments. Hal found himself pulled into the hunt for government services, even though he'd hoped that the Bluefield Union Mission would do more of the legwork. With the mission staff busy helping the vast clientele that phoned or walked in seeking aid, Jesse-Ray's needs weren't always high on the staff's priority list.

In the down time between Jesse-Ray's appointments and during the evenings, Jesse-Ray talked, and Hal listened. They would talk on the phone in the morning before Jesse-Ray went to work at the mission. They would talk in waiting rooms at social-service agency buildings. And Hal was especially solicitous at the end of every day, letting Jesse-Ray unburden himself for as long as he wanted to, even if it meant standing out in the driveway for an hour when all Hal wanted to do was go inside to sit down.

Hal retold Jesse-Ray's stories to me over the phone every night. Tales emerged of a troubled childhood and the chaotic life of an abused and abandoned child-turned-teenage meth-cook. Stories of his violent biological father who lived on the outskirts of the law, complemented by tales of a gangland father figure named Rick, began to take shape, giving us a glimpse of Jesse-Ray's primary role models. Jesse-Ray had learned nothing about kindness and little about responsibility from his father, and Rick's influence further cemented Jesse-Ray's view of himself as a person suited for life on the margins, with criminality as the most promising career path.

Hal overflowed with sympathy for Jesse-Ray, believing everything the young man said. I could see Hal's heart go out to him as he took on Jesse-Ray's struggles as his own.

After all, Jesse-Ray was a kid with no real mother, and everyone seemed to know this about him. When he was growing up, he overheard people discussing it. Other kids asked him about her absence. Because of this maternal lack, he always felt different. A big question mark hovered over his head. How could a kid have no mom? Where had she gone?

My first inkling that Jesse-Ray could be an effective storyteller came during one of our early conversations when he touched on a seminal incident involving his mother's past. It happened at a hospital when he was eleven or twelve, soon after he went into foster care. His foster mother had a biological son old enough to be employed, and this son had a job at the hospital.

One day she and Jesse-Ray dropped the older boy off for his shift, and the foster mother remembered that she needed to get some sort of records relating to Jesse-Ray. Perhaps she needed Jesse-Ray's birth or vaccination records to enroll him in school. His memory was hazy, and he couldn't remember the exact nature of her errand.

But, unknown to her, Jesse-Ray also sought something. Standing in the lobby of the hospital, Jesse-Ray decided to investigate a mystery that had always plagued him. Why didn't he have a mother? His father never gave an adequate explanation. Jesse-Ray had been told his mother was an addict who'd abandoned him, but he felt like he was the boy people always whispered about. It suddenly occurred to Jesse-Ray that he could get answers by talking to the doctor who'd delivered him.

"I needed to talk to the dude who grabbed me by the legs and pulled me out," explained Jesse-Ray in his typical colorful-but-spare phrasing.

As he related what happened at the hospital that day, his descriptions were peppered with obscenities that marked his conversational style, which plagued Hal, who tried to ban them, but which I never discouraged. I didn't want anything to restrain Jesse-Ray's imagination. Even at his most vulgar, his way of speaking could make you root for him.

At the hospital, he desperately wanted answers, and the desk clerk was either lazy or indifferent. He wanted her to consult the records, to look up the names of the medical professionals who were in the room when he was born. She refused. He disparaged her attitude and her looks. When it became clear that she "didn't want to move her ass" on his behalf, Jesse-Ray insisted, "Fuck you. Do it!"

As that rude imperative came out of his mouth, his foster mother sprang into action, which Jesse-Ray described as "the first time my foster mother smacked the shit out of me."

But Jesse-Ray didn't care about his stinging scalp. He just wanted answers. Once the records were located, he left his foster mother and the desk clerk behind and rode the elevator to talk to someone. A medic? A doctor? A technician? Jesse-Ray had no idea who this person was. He was someone who had attended Jesse-Ray's birth or at least had access to records of the event.

Silently, the man printed out a list. "I just kinda ripped it out of his hands," Jesse-Ray told me. "I saw everything I already knew." The printout listed every drug he'd ever heard of. Meth, coke, and more. He asked nothing more of the man who printed out the list, and the man volunteered nothing else. Jesse-Ray headed back down to the lobby.

I asked, "If you could choose between meth and coke, for just one of those drugs to be in your system when you were born, which one would it be?"

He pondered before answering. "That's like saying, would you rather be set on fire or stabbed to death?"

Comebacks like that were one reason I grew to love Jesse-Ray so much. He had a way of cutting through the banana oil.

The hard-luck outlines of Jesse-Ray's life were real. Yet I sensed that nothing good would come from Hal becoming an overeager advocate. Because of the advice and training I'd received from addiction professionals when my own child, then about Jesse-Ray's age, was in recovery, I was aware of the dangers. Hal was beginning to look like a classic enabler.

Hal's obligation was to leave it up to Jesse-Ray to face reality and suffer the consequences of his actions, especially if he failed to live up to his minimal responsibilities during his workdays at the Bluefield Union Mission. Instead Hal let his sympathies stand in the way of setting common-sense rules. During their chats, he allowed Jesse-Ray to fixate on his problems and dwell on his self-defeating attitudes rather than try to steer his thinking in productive directions. Hal tolerated bad behavior such as Jesse-Ray's refusing to get out of bed on time. What's more, Hal began to make excuses for Jesse-Ray.

For instance, I recommended that Jesse-Ray listen to a YouTube recording of a lecture from the 1960s by Joel S. Goldsmith, author of *The Infinite Way* book series. I searched for it on Jesse-Ray's computer, and he bookmarked it, so he could listen to it at his convenience. I offered the suggestion as uplifting material to replace Jesse-Ray's negative thoughts, which he'd described as nonstop and enslaving. I hoped he'd become ennobled and better able to shake off his depressive ruminations after listening to Goldsmith's compelling lecture about man's spiritual identity.

Maybe it was unrealistic to expect that a scrappy nineteen-year-old would be interested in a mystic from the previous century. Yet I believed Goldsmith's perspective—that the five human senses are not accurate depicters of a person's true nature and that divine help is always at the ready, as long as it is realized in consciousness— would lift Jesse-Ray's mood. In my view, he was mired in mental misery, seeing no way out. Hal saw my point and told Jesse-Ray he'd sit together with him to listen to the tape. Every couple of weeks I asked Hal if they'd done it. Every time, he said that Jesse-Ray had refused. He couldn't possibly sit still for a lecture, Hal said. He lacked the patience and attention span. I didn't know which was worse—Jesse-Ray's ignoring my suggestion or Hal's excuses for his behavior.

I cautioned Hal to be skeptical about Jesse-Ray's descriptions of gangland living. We wouldn't do Jesse-Ray any favors by believing his stories of bloody drug-running if they were little more than tall tales. Our job was to help Jesse-Ray see reality, not be a party to any fantasy past he may have concocted to make himself seem important. My training as a journalist kicked in when some of his tales seemed outlandish.

I believed kernels of truth existed in all of his stories, but at the same time, I knew he was capable of embellishment. He had told me that when he first appealed to the Bluefield Union Mission for help, he claimed to have been in the military because he'd heard rumors that the mission always helped veterans. Jesse-Ray was never in the military.

"We shouldn't believe anything Jesse-Ray says unless we can verify it," I said to Hal.

Eventually Hal acquired paperwork that backed up key parts of Jesse-Ray's life story, such as his arrest record, school transcripts, and foster-care tenure. Hal and Jesse-Ray contacted the high school and requested transcripts. They tracked down Jesse-Ray's former social worker and spoke to her on the phone, requesting that she mail the documents he needed to prove that he was eligible for services and to enroll in college, which she did. At the beginning we knew only what he told us. I was always eager to hear more.

Jesse-Ray's flair for storytelling had been apparent at our first meeting when he had talked about working in the coal mine and worrying about the roof over his head. Every weekend that I was in town, I sat him down to record details of his life, and we fashioned these experiences into a poem. And then another and another. He began to write drafts at home, alone, late at night. Our writing connection developed during the work week even though we couldn't meet face to face; he sent drafts via email, using the computer we'd provided. He said he couldn't believe that anyone would want to read his writing, but he was willing to open his life to the world if telling his story could help someone else.

But it was actually Hal who deserved the credit for discovering Jesse-Ray's writing proclivity. One day, he'd spotted a crumpled ball of paper on the kitchen floor of the safe house. Jesse-Ray said it was nothing, just him jotting down his thoughts, then throwing them away. Hal smoothed out the paper. He had no way of judging whether Jesse-Ray's scribblings had literary merit. But he was insistent that Jesse-Ray stop trashing them. "You'll want to read these someday," he said. "They'll mean a lot to you." He urged Jesse-Ray to share his writings with me, sparking our literary partnership.

Hal also coached Jesse-Ray in the routines of daily life such as showering and showing up on time at the Bluefield Union Mission and for any appointments. He urged Jesse-Ray to exhibit a good attitude and willingness to be helpful during his volunteer shifts. Hal stressed to Jesse-Ray the value of the poetry that he was composing. Hal, who'd been told he was stupid when his learning disabilities went undiagnosed throughout his school years, counseled Jesse-Ray that his aptitude for writing was something to be prized. "You can do something that I, in a million years, could never do," Hal said, praising Jesse-Ray's talent to boost his confidence. He prepared him for the idea that I would want to talk with him on weekends. I would be looking for the details about his life. These details were vital to creating the content that would go into his chapbook of poetry. Jesse-Ray was highly skeptical that his poems were worthy of being published. This was clearly a novel idea to him. But both Hal and I, excited about his abilities, assured him his talent was real.

Despite Hal's pep talks, Jesse-Ray seemed dubious about answering questions while I took notes. I never had to "force" Jesse-Ray to write. He wrote all the time—always had. I saw my role as mentor, steering him toward subject matter that would appeal to a broad audience. Sitting across from me on our living room couch, he was quiet until my questions opened floodgates. Even though I expected stories of a tough childhood, nothing could have prepared me for the details. And even though some of Jesse-Ray's stories of wealth and adventure with drug gangs seemed incredible, much of what he said about his home life had the ring of truth.

During one conversation that lasted for two hours, I choked back tears over what the child had endured. Tears do not come easily to me. I had a newspaper career that had spanned twenty-five years—I was a reporter for the *Tampa Times*, an editorial writer for the *Tampa Tribune*, an editorial page editor for the *Tallahassee Democrat*, and editor of the *Weekly Planet* alternative newspaper in Sarasota, Florida. I had countless hours of on-the-job training in how not to show emotion that might interrupt an interaction or spook an interviewee. I've interviewed convicted child abusers, political gadflies, high-profile Native American activists, and people momentarily famous like Regina Twigg, the woman whose baby was deliberately switched at birth for another infant in a Florida hospital. Rapport is essential to keep the subject talking. With difficulty, I kept a neutral expression, drawing out his story as fast as he and I could stand it. I suspected Jesse-Ray would clam up in the face of a surprised, judgmental, or sad response.

Sometimes I used the ploy of a bathroom break or some other quick chore to steady my emotions. At other times, Jesse-Ray's own reactions to these turbulent memories would bring his monologue to a standstill, and he would have to calm himself—usually by going outside to smoke—before continuing.

Jesse-Ray professed to remember little from early childhood, which made sense; if he had endured horrific trials, repressed memories would be both a blessing and a survival mechanism. He claimed his earliest memory was of a rape taking place beside him on a mattress. He knew both the perpetrator and the victim.

He said that he, himself, might have been raped. Later, he amended this admission to say, without equivocation, that he *was* raped. As our work on the book of poetry continued, he acknowledged the sexual violence in his own words, spelling out both the incident and its effect on his psyche: "Part of me wants to trust, but I was raped." The purpose of our conversations was for Jesse-Ray to be honest about his memories and to turn the painful ones into an artistic statement.

Even at the start, I recognized that Jesse-Ray's probing of his past—with no psychiatrist on hand or drugs, legal or otherwise, to numb the painful memories—could come at a cost. He had told Hal that he didn't completely understand why I wanted to ask him so many questions. Spending Saturday and Sunday afternoons being interrogated wasn't an activity that made sense to Jesse-Ray.

I tried to make my reasoning clear as well.

"This is going to be difficult, dredging up all these events," I told him. "But I think the payoff will be worth it. People will want to read your story, even learn from it."

He looked at me, cocking his head like an exotic bird. "You mean someone might get something out of my life?" His expression was perplexed.

"Absolutely. To hear how you've suffered and yet forged ahead—that's inspiring!"

"I don't see how." His voice took on a higher timbre as uncertainty crept in.

"When you tell your story, people will see that you survived. Not only have you survived and been open about what you suffered, but you've also overcome your past. You asked for help. You're building a new life. And now, you could be a published author. People will see that if you can accomplish things, they can, too."

Jesse-Ray shook his head. The prospect of becoming an author was beyond his imagining. At this point I had no publisher and no contract to prove there would be a book at the end of the process. But he went along with my judgment that his experiences growing up in Appalachia would fascinate readers. He liked the idea of putting out a book under his name. He still suffered from lack of self-confidence and belief that his work was unworthy.

As we went over the bare facts to establish context and time frames, I could see that dredging up childhood memories was unpleasant for him, though he tried to be tough. Sometimes he'd pause for a long moment if a question threw him. An expression of pain would flicker on his face before he could regain composure. I feared that the memories might prey on his mind and indeed, in time, they did.

Ever the naturally talented writer, he tried to come up with metaphors to make me understand his early life.

"First, I have to explain to you what a trap house is," he said one Saturday afternoon. Jesse-Ray perched on the camel-colored leather couch in our living room as I sat on a red leather chair across from him. A wooden chest that Hal had stained to show its wood grain sat between us, decorated with an assortment of handmade ceramic bowls. Looking around our living room, Jesse-Ray had surmised that I probably didn't know what a trap house was. He was right. The term was new to me.

"People in a trap house come and go at all hours," he said, explaining that drugs were bought and sold in trap houses.

Jesse-Ray grew up in a trap house. Everyone around him was stoned all the time. The only person who showed him any tenderness was his grandmother, the woman Jesse-Ray called "Mom" or "Mama." But she didn't talk much.

"She cried, mostly," he said.

"Why?"

"Because of what her life was like."

She had been raped as a child. She was also a heavy drug user. Virtually all that Jesse-Ray knew about his childhood was from what his grandmother (his father's mother) told him.

His grandmother also suffered at the hand of Jesse-Ray's father. Jesse-Ray saw it happen. He could have called an abuse hotline or talked to someone at school to report domestic violence or child abuse. But even though his grandmother was getting hurt, Jesse-Ray would never turn in the perpetrator. In Jesse-Ray's world, talking to police and judges was an unforgivable sin. I stopped taking notes to pose a question.

"What if another child might be in danger because the perpetrator is free to commit violence again?" I asked him.

"If I thought he would hurt another child, I'd take care of him myself," Jesse-Ray replied. He tilted his head back, tensing his jaw in a gesture that implied sullen determination.

In his early childhood, Jesse-Ray's grandmother was his sun, moon, and stars. Later, she would die in his arms.

It might seem curious, but Jesse-Ray's rape, which he referred to matter-of-factly as if buying a soda, did not bring me to tears. Rather, what seemed unbearably sweet and sad to me was the way his grandmother once comforted him in the night.

Almost always, they slept together on a mattress on the floor. He couldn't understand why there was no bed or bedside table or cozy stuffed chair. Just a mattress on the floor. "We couldn't afford anything else for some fuckin' reason," he said.

In one searing memory, he was awake and cold in the dark of night. His grandmother told him to think about *Little House on the Prairie*.

"I had no fuckin' idea what that was," he said. "But it made me feel warm inside." Soothed, he fell back to sleep.

It was heartbreaking, that detail—a child surrounded by adults so self-centered or disinterested or imprisoned or stoned that he was never introduced to the iconic *Little House on the Prairie*. Not only that, but he didn't remember a grown-up ever reading him a book. As he talked, I felt like I'd been stabbed in the eyes. My mother read the Laura Ingalls Wilder books aloud to me and my siblings when we were little, back in the fifties and sixties, even before the stories entered the American cultural lexicon via television.

While his grandmother comforted him by evoking the title, he had no idea that *Little House on the Prairie* represented a loving family whose members looked out for each other.

Similarly, he didn't remember an adult ever cooking him a meal. I pressed him to recall his favorite food from childhood. He said he couldn't. But one recipe stood out. It was called "bitter potatoes." His grandmother told him that he first sampled this delicacy when he was three. She never spared the gory details when she filled in the pictures of his toddlerhood.

What made the potatoes bitter? They were laced with Xanax. With a little half-grin cutting his broad face, Jesse-Ray said he liked them even better when he got older.

When Jesse-Ray talked about his childhood, the conversations seemed to go on forever, and I felt like I was trapped in a horror movie that had no break in the suspense. Just when I thought I'd heard the most abhorrent thing imaginable, Jesse-Ray would recount some other awful incident.

The hardest thing to hear was about his cousin Zach, who was three years older than Jesse-Ray. Unlike Jesse-Ray, whose father never let him leave the house, Zach got to go places. Jesse-Ray didn't understand why he couldn't leave the house. It was just the way things were. His father's word was law.

I surmised that Jesse-Ray's father didn't want to take the chance of a kid running around the neighborhood yapping about things going on in the trap house. If Jesse-Ray's recollections were true, it stood to reason that his father didn't want attention drawn to his lifestyle or abode.

Zach was not constrained by such rules. Zach was a free-range kid. Zach knew about the world. Zach taught Jesse-Ray things.

Jesse-Ray loved Zach.

However, according to Jesse-Ray, Zach didn't have loving parents. Zach had been told he was a "mistake," a child who hadn't been planned and shouldn't have been born. In response, Zach impressed Jesse-Ray with an obsession with death. Zach wanted to die and articulated his death wish in dramatic and poetic ways; he rhapsodized about it. In the woods, he'd find dead animals and roll in their stench. He wanted to take that smell with him into his own bedroom. He wanted to smell death continually.

"I miss Zach so much," Jesse-Ray said. He rarely made statements that showed how he felt, so I was glad to hear him convey the intensity of missing his cousin. Teenage males famously shy away from sharing their feelings, and Jesse-Ray's drug use had disrupted his connection to his emotions. He said that most of the time, he felt nothing but numb. I wasn't surprised to hear this because recovering addicts often report the same challenge.

What's more, the poetry he was writing was laced with images of vomit and blood and barbed wire, images far removed from any positive human connection. When he spoke about his father and grandmother, his language seemed tempered, if not guarded. In contrast, when he spoke about Zach, his eyes lit up, and he openly expressed sentiments akin to joy. I liked hearing about this boyhood friendship that had touched him deeply.

The conclusion of the Zach story was deceptively simple: Zach died in a house fire. But there was more to it.

In Jesse-Ray's mind, the origins of the fire were murky. He had heard people telling varying stories of who might have started it, who might've known about it, and who might've saved Zach— but didn't. In one version of events, Zach himself might've been responsible for the flames.

I struggled to keep composed as Jesse-Ray spoke about this

young boy who felt unloved, who craved death, who died in tortuous and suspicious circumstances. Jesse-Ray's voice rose in pitch as he talked about Zach, and I could only imagine the effect of the loss on his emerging character.

Zach was only thirteen. That would have made Jesse-Ray just ten years old when he lost his cousin and best friend.

In a family devoid of *Little House on the Prairie* books or reruns, none of the adults were capable of comforting Jesse-Ray. I suspected that they probably didn't even recognize his suffering. Certainly no one got on the phone to line up grief counseling to help Jesse-Ray cope.

I fought a lump in my throat as soon as I realized that the story would end with Zach's death, but Jesse-Ray seemed surprisingly unmoved in the retelling. Maybe he was so numb that horror no longer found purchase, at least not during daylight hours. (A few weeks later, nightmares beset him, and his grandmother appeared to him as a horrifying apparition.) Jesse-Ray was stone cold as he told Zach's story, but no such numbness protected me. An overarching sense of vicarious grief clung to me for hours.

A couple of weeks after hearing about Zach's death, I sat down with Jesse-Ray for another interview, and after an hour we trod on territory that once again involved betrayal and loss. This time it was Jesse-Ray who was overcome with emotion during the recounting.

He sat on the same spot on the living room couch, perched across from me as we pieced together parts of his teenage life. He described being evicted from his father's trailer because of a landlord's edict. He grew indignant in telling me the story because, in his mind, an injustice had occurred. Anger welled inside him, and he threw himself out the front door and down the stone porch steps.

Five minutes later, he was back, eyes shining, flashing that bright Jesse-Ray grin. He told me he'd just punched a tree and showed me his scraped knuckles. He was proud of himself, having channeled his anger in ways that didn't involve pummeling other humans. He was calm and civilized, ready to sit down again and face my questions.

As he sent me draft after draft of verse, I grew more convinced that Jesse-Ray's colorful use of language, dramatic past, and willingness to bare his soul were a winning combination. His poems came together via one of two methods: either I would edit the lines he would write at night and email to me, or I would arrange words he'd said during our conversations into lines and stanzas. My conviction was strong: Jesse-Ray could become a writer with a following. Even modest fame as a writer could propel Jesse-Ray from poverty, replace the drug highs with purpose and meaning, and keep him from repeating the cycles of poverty, addiction, and abuse. I was a believer.

Hal didn't have the background to assess Jesse-Ray's talents, but he didn't doubt my instincts. He agreed that Jesse-Ray's writing ability was an asset for the young man to build on. Even if Jesse-Ray didn't buy into the idea of writing as a career, his ability to communicate would help him succeed in college. There seemed to be no downside to encouraging Jesse-Ray to think deeply about his past and turn those thoughts into self-expression.

His output showed flashes of brilliance, and I couldn't bear the thought of it staying hidden from the world. Like Hal, I was sad about all those scraps of paper Jesse-Ray had balled up and thrown away. He'd discarded his poetry, treating it like trash, as if nothing about his heart and soul carried value.

I was eager for Jesse-Ray to witness how his story might not only transform his own life but also become a valuable addition to literature about homelessness, child abuse, drug addiction, and the lure of gangs. Many positive things could spring from publication of Jesse-Ray's poetry, including a sense of accomplishment like nothing he'd ever experienced. In my mind, these potential advantages outweighed the pain Jesse-Ray felt as he unearthed and examined his memories. Success, praise, and accolades would balance out the agony and eventual nightmares resulting from the artistic expressions taking shape during the birth process of his book, *Hillbilly Drug Baby: The Poems*. Or so I believed.

Incest in Appalachia

"I was raped," Jesse-Ray Lewis wrote in a poem. Despite having few memories of early childhood, his memories of rape persisted.

Stereotypes about incest in Appalachia abound, having entered popular culture, sometimes in dismissive ways that indiscriminately tar the region's residents.

A Midwestern woman, whose childhood trauma led her to become an advocate for sexually abused children, says her father justified his repeated rapes of her by saying, "A lot of fathers and daughters have this kind of relationship. They do it in the Appalachian district all the time."

Several studies going back at least to 1985 show that Appalachia's domestic violence and incest rates are higher than national averages. In 1991, Peggy Cantrell, an associate professor at East Tennessee State University, told the Associated Press, "We're supposed to be a very family-oriented society. But traditional family values may include strong authority and strict discipline, including violent punishment. That's a very ingrained, traditional value. The Appalachian family is still patriarchal. The dominance of the father, combined with isolation and a close-knit family, can lead to more domestic violence and incest."

Estimates of the prevalence of rape, physical violence, and/ or stalking by an intimate partner range from 17.4 percent to 41.2 percent in a state-by-state comparison, with West Virginia having the highest proportion of people in any state with a history of sexual violence, according to a federal government survey. Rounding out other states in south and central Appalachia, Tennessee's proportion is 32.5 percent, Kentucky's 31 percent, Ohio's 30 percent, and Virginia's 22.1 percent. (Jesse-Ray's experiences took place in Virginia near the West Virginia border.)

A battered wife in West Virginia recounts stealing away to the family barn and taking comfort in the warmth of a longhaired ewe. Cuddling the farm animal brought back happy childhood memories of shearing sheep. At that time, seeking help from a women's shelter was out of the question. Another impediment to escape was the rugged, mile-long driveway connecting her family home to the main road. This same woman later undertook graduate studies of domestic violence in Appalachia and wrote about cultural barriers, which included "a mistrust of outsiders, fear of the 'system,' a tradition of self-sufficiency and taking care of one's own, and of social isolation."

Jesse-Ray's self-described isolation included being forbidden to leave the home after school and on weekends, and his experience of other children's mothers pointing him out to their offspring, warning them not to be like him.

The Centers for Disease Control reports that more than a quarter of boys are ten years old or younger at the time of their first rape. Almost 10 percent of child abuse cases are reports of sexual abuse, with almost 60,000 children suffering sexual abuse each year.

The American Society for the Positive Care of Children lists other facts and figures about child sexual abuse, including:

- Most perpetrators are men (96 percent);

- One in six boys will be sexually abused before the age of eighteen; and

- One-third of perpetrators are family members.

In addition, drug or alcohol abuse by the caregiver puts a child at much higher risk for sexual abuse.

The upshot? Research shows that as adults, sexually abused children are likely to experience psychological problems including post-traumatic stress syndrome, depression, suicide, substance abuse, and relationship problems. They are also more likely to drop out of school.

Most of these issues—including thoughts of suicide—surfaced in Jesse-Ray's life during the five-and-a-half months he was associated with the Bluefield Union Mission.

The American Society for the Positive Care of Children recommends its Darkness to Light adult education program as a way "to empower adults through awareness and educational programs to prevent, recognize, and react responsibly to child sexual abuse." A guide to preventing abuse, "5 Steps to Protecting Our Children," and a training program called Stewards of Children, can be found at the website www.d2l.org/education/.

CHAPTER 3

Hal and Jesse-Ray revisit the abandoned house

I'm not looking for pity
but inner divinity.

Are we
human beings
(a not-so-perfect
bundle of atoms)
trying to fuck over everything?

—Jesse-Ray Lewis, "Forgive Me"

Hal is a hobby photographer. Shortly after Jesse-Ray arrived on our doorstep, the two of them went on a photo shoot to document the place where he'd been living before he moved into the safe house. For a few weeks, he had slept outdoors off Bluefield Avenue no more than a three-minute drive from the Bluefield Union Mission. Jesse-Ray had arrived by bus with just a few dollars in his pocket.

During his first few days in Bluefield, only the branches of a tree provided shelter. Jesse-Ray had arrived by bus with just a few dollars in his pocket.

But as he began to panhandle and leverage his begging booty to finance a petty drug-dealing operation (supporting himself via the one trade he knew—illegal drugs), he took up digs in an abandoned house nearby.

Hal photographed the depression under the tree where Jesse-

Ray slept, a hollowed-out spot where Jesse-Ray had laid his sleeping bag. The scraped dirt looked like a nest, a spot of earth that feral hogs might trample or a shady patch that deer might favor for a nap.

A blue bucket sat near the tree. Jesse-Ray joked that the bucket was his easy chair. Hal photographed Jesse-Ray sitting on the upside-down plastic bucket, having a smoke. The resulting photo had an iconic look, an illustration of Appalachian poverty summed up in a single image.

The abandoned house that Jesse-Ray had stayed in was a couple of hundred yards away from the tree, its cement walls cracked and crumbling, window glass long shattered and scattered. Enough of a structure remained to break whipping winds on cold evenings and keep a person mostly dry against the rain and snow.

Bluefield abounds with abandoned houses. Our neighborhood was no exception, consisting of mostly two-story houses built in the 1920s, many of which had fallen into disrepair. Similar blight could be seen up and down Bluefield Avenue, including on the Virginia side of the state line about two miles from our house, where Jesse-Ray had taken up residence. Economic decline had infected not just the two Bluefields but also much of West Virginia and Southwest Virginia, including the tiny neighboring coal towns of Harman, Pocahontas, and War. Coal mined in Pocahontas was spectacularly clean, burning with little or no smoke produced under combustion, and it was crucial to the operation of the US Navy during both world wars. The coal and railroad barons, millionaires all, lived in the smaller town of Bramwell about six miles from Bluefield, next door to Pocahontas. Many of the mansions there, too, are now decrepit, though some have been lavishly restored.

In the late 1800s, Bluefield prospered as a center for the railroad transport of coal, and homes sprang up to house working and middle-class families. During that time, wood was plentiful in the region, providing gorgeous raw material for floors, staircases, and oak-trimmed windows. However, like other Appalachian towns,

Bluefield grappled with an economic decline during the middle of the previous century. By 1950, the coal boom was over, and by 1960, thousands of miners had been thrown out of work. Not only had many of the mines been depleted, but also the industry had become mechanized, rendering workers' jobs obsolete.

Downtown Bluefield, West Virginia, a once-thriving community rich with railroad history and famous for its Art Deco buildings, had become a sorry site of spectacular building collapses. Three significant buildings had fallen since Hal and I had moved to Bluefield in 2007. In 2009, the Matz Hotel, built in 1911, crashed to the ground. The old Colonial Theater beside it met the sidewalk as well. Two years earlier, the former People's Bank Building—the oldest brownstone south of Charleston, West Virginia's capital—had crumpled into chunks and shards.

Hal and I were shocked that our adopted city could allow its architectural history to disappear so ignominiously. We began to understand how little money and few resources the town possessed, despite the half dozen or so fabulously wealthy families who'd lived here since the turn of the last century.

Bluefield's residential housing stock was hardly more inspiring. Sun-bleached wooden houses sagged until they finally crumbled under their own weight. Decrepit structures resembling horror-movie habitats were overgrown with vines as gravity defeated their rotting porches and posts. In a city with a population of barely 10,000, a full-time demolition crew was kept busy bulldozing the sagging structures that scarred the landscape, but the list of condemned buildings remained in the hundreds, and the goal of eliminating this neighborhood blight seemed impossible. The city had already razed three houses within a block or two of our home, but more remained. It was no surprise that Jesse-Ray had stumbled upon an empty structure whose concrete walls afforded him a measure of shelter.

The pair poked around the property, Hal asking Jesse-Ray to pose on the grounds as well as inside the rundown shell. Jesse-

Ray looked good in photos. His straight nose, open expression, and long-lashed eyes made for flattering portraits, and the hint of rebelliousness in his expression added interest. Hal photographed Jesse-Ray in the abandoned house in silhouette. He sat on a window ledge in the dark building, looking out toward the sunny day. He cut a solitary profile, face mostly in shadow, a figure equidistant between two worlds, light and dark. It was not yet clear which of the worlds he'd succumb to, which gravitational pull would triumph.

After the photo session, they walked through the house together, inspecting one room after the next. They found a red bag on the floor—the bag Jesse-Ray had stashed his drugs in for around-town delivery. Jesse-Ray scooped up the empty receptacle to take home and add to his meager possessions at the safe house.

As they were standing outside, Jesse-Ray made a startling admission to Hal: In his former life, he had packed heat. He had left his gun on these premises.

Jesse-Ray explained that when one leaves a gang, one must bury the gun deep in the earth. The burial ritual was a symbolic act of severance.

Hal, being a man of good instincts, wanted to dig it up and do whatever a law-abiding citizen should legally do with a cast-off weapon. Or, at the very least, find it and chop it to pieces so it could no longer be employed to do harm. But Jesse-Ray was adamant, refusing to lead Hal to the buried firearm because unearthing a gun was bad luck. Even more important, digging up a gun violated an unbreakable rule of gang life—one never digs up a gun after one has buried it. According to Jesse-Ray, the gun must stay where he had planted it beneath the topsoil.

Hal didn't need to ask if the gun was involved in crimes. Jesse-Ray had already said enough about his meth-cooking days to convey which side of the law he had lived on. Being involved in a drug gang meant retaliating against snitches, customers who didn't pay, rival gang members, and other lowlifes. And if someone got caught in the path of a bullet, that was just the price of being in the life.

Despite the criminal violence of his recent past, Jesse-Ray shrugged off the fact that the gun could be used as ammunition against him in court. He didn't seem afraid that the gun might be found and could tie him to the crimes and shootings he'd told us about. In fact, he claimed that the firearm was not only devoid of fingerprints, but also untraceable in every other way. He declared little respect for the law. His sole concern had been adhering to a set of gang rules.

He also told Hal that there was one more reason to leave the gun buried. He wanted nothing more to do with it. He didn't want to hurt anyone. He wanted to forget, to leave it all behind.

The sun sank, and it was time for them to go. Jesse-Ray patted his pants. Somehow the black gang flag had gone missing. For a moment, Jesse-Ray thought he might have lost it. He grew frantic, refusing to leave. Hal recounted later that Jesse-Ray's distress was palpable.

They scoured the house and grounds and found it on the earth near the tree. Only when the gang flag was back in his possession did Jesse-Ray shake off his agitation.

Apparently, some things couldn't be buried or left behind.

Poverty in Appalachia

More than six hundred coal mines closed in Central Appalachia in the early 1990s after the fossil fuel-based industry entered its final death spasms. Furniture manufacturing and textile industry jobs also fled the region over the past two decades—a region whose people suffered from malignant stereotypes even before its poverty famously shocked John F. Kennedy during the 1960 presidential campaign.

West Virginia's McDowell County was once the nation's so-called coal bin. According to USA Today, it is now "a socioeconomic disaster area where 70 percent of children live in a household without a working adult, and 46 percent live with neither biological parent." The county's population plummeted from 71,000 to 21,000 during the decades since Kennedy's visit.

The same sad economic story has played out across Central and Southern Appalachia. Everywhere one looks, the poverty rate is above the national average. Two places mentioned in the news recently include, first, Beattyville, Kentucky, where more than half of the population lives below the poverty line, making it one of the half-dozen poorest towns in America of more than a thousand people; and, second, the county once home to the Westmoreland Coal Company, Wise County, Virginia, with a poverty rate of 22.4 percent, compared with the US national rate of between 13 and 14 percent.

"The state with the worst poverty rate in the region is Kentucky with a 25.4 percent rate in the Appalachian portion versus 18.9 percent rate for the rest of the state," reports FAHE, a group dedicated to eliminating poverty in Appalachia. "In 2014, the per capita income of the Appalachian region of Kentucky was only $30,308 while the entire United States was at $46,049."

Many communities have withstood a double whammy of economic and environmental loss. Coal impoundments hold billions of gallons of toxic waste created from coal mining. Failures of these large, hazardous dams have caused spectacular environmental catastrophes such as the impoundment break in 1972 that killed 125 people in West Virginia and a disaster in 2000 that poisoned waterways in Kentucky with more than 300 million gallons of slurry (an amount thirty times larger than the Exxon Valdez oil spill).

Adding insult to injury, a Washington State University researcher has found that neighborhoods situated near coal impoundments in Appalachia are "more likely to have higher rates of poverty and unemployment. Coal mining makes up a small percentage of the region's jobs but threatens local communities through the creation of environmental hazards."

What created the status quo? For context in understanding Appalachia's economic decline, writer Scott Rodd reflects on the region's history:

"Historically, Appalachia consisted of discrete, tight-knit communities that were self-sufficient and self-sustaining. Local agriculture and tradesmen served nearby residents, and communities lost few members to the outside world. These trends continued through the 19th century, but the world around Appalachia began to drastically change during the following century and eventually outpaced the region's ability to adapt."

Writing about poverty in Appalachia can be controversial, as TV journalist Diane Sawyer discovered while promoting the 2009 documentary "The Hidden America—Children of the Mountains." Many viewers were livid and far less restrained in their criticism than West Virginian B.L. Dotson Lewis, who wrote in the Daily Yonder blog: "For one hour the screen was filled with down-and-out families where drugs, missing teeth, filthy living conditions, shabby housing, litter, and lack of food made me ashamed. Was I ashamed because I, too, come from Appalachia or because poverty is a truth in our region? I couldn't answer. I was glued to the set even though I had a good idea where this was going."

How to turn the tide? Individual responsibility? Government aid?

"Yes, I worked hard, but I didn't just pull myself up by my bootstraps," writes Betsy Rader in a Washington Post opinion piece. After a childhood living in poverty with three siblings and raised by a single mother, she encountered a school guidance counselor who encouraged her to go to college, using scholarships and subsidized federal loans to pay her way. Arguing against the thesis of J.D. Vance's bestselling book *Hillbilly Elegy*, she concludes, "Life, liberty, and the pursuit of happiness should be legitimate expectations for everyone, 'hillbillies' included."

If Appalachia's natural beauty is its rainbow, millennials might be considered its pot of gold. Southwest Virginia is celebrating a tiny uptick in the percentage of college-educated adults aged 25 to 34 living in the region—from 2.3 percent in 2000 to 3.04 percent in 2015. The collaborative efforts of governments, nonprofits, and businesses to promote outdoor recreation along with music and the arts has been credited for this positive demographic shift.

CHAPTER 4

Go directly to jail

My girlfriend
fights her demons.
I cradle mine.
Try to hide
but there's no hiding.

—Jesse-Ray Lewis, "Demons"

S oon after arriving in Bluefield, Jesse-Ray mentioned there was a court case hanging over his head in a rural county in Virginia where he'd spent some of his high-school years. Without any transport to the courthouse (at least this was his excuse), he'd missed the designated date to meet up with his court-appointed lawyer to appear before a judge.

In typical Jesse-Ray fashion, he was foggy about the crime, the circumstance, and the consequences. He couldn't even remember the last name of his attorney.

Clearly, he was anxious about having skipped out on the charges. He didn't necessarily want to make good on the situation, but he was distressed enough to bring it up with Hal. Hal was his confidant, and it was understandable that he would turn to Hal, rather than anyone at the Bluefield Union Mission, for help. The mission was a frenetic place, with staff members working at a steady pace to help hundreds of residents meet their basic needs. No one at the mission was as focused on Jesse-Ray's problems as Hal and me, so it fell to us to delve deeper.

Jesse-Ray made it clear to Hal that he was not in favor of taking action. He wanted to ignore the situation and, hopefully, stay far enough under the radar that police would never pick him up again.

Hal stood firm, trying to reason with Jesse-Ray. "You've got to get this behind you," he said.

He argued that for Jesse-Ray to start a new life, he would need to face the consequences of his actions. Only when he had laid the legal matter to rest could he forge ahead and set new goals. "You can't go through life looking over your shoulder," Hal said. "One traffic stop, and you'll be off to prison."

When I came home for the weekend and got wind of the problem, I spent Saturday evening scouring court records. The Internet spit out the particulars of his arrest. It was true: In Virginia, in a town about an hour and a half away from Bluefield, the justice system had logged a drug crime in Jesse-Ray's name.

But there was more.

He had missed not one, but two court dates, and his final date to appear had been on Friday, just one day before! Had he showed up in court just thirty-six hours earlier, this criminal matter might have been dispensed with. As things stood, Jesse-Ray was a fugitive.

From the court records, I unearthed the name of his court-appointed attorney and wrote a page of details that Hal could take down to the Bluefield Union Mission the following Monday morning. Hal and I agreed that if the residence we owned harbored a fugitive, we didn't want to deal with the situation alone. Moreover, the rehabilitation of this aged-out foster child was a joint project between us and the mission. It seemed like a good time to tap them for help. Plus, the court system would probably take more serious notice if contacted by a representative of the Bluefield Union Mission. Hal and I were private citizens with no standing to interfere in Jesse-Ray's life—much less any judicial proceedings.

The attorney's name would offer a place to start. It would give Craig Hammond, the mission's executive director, someone to talk to about how to proceed. The court records stated the initial charge: possession of marijuana. Jesse-Ray would also be forced to answer to the charge of being on the run from the law.

Oddly, having openly regaled us with his drug dealing experiences and details of his many unlawful acts, Jesse-Ray maintained his innocence of the pot-possession charge.

"It wasn't even mine!" he protested.

We didn't know what to think.

Jesse-Ray had been eighteen at the time of the charge. He explained that his foster parents had pinned the crime on him after they found marijuana on his bed.

"I didn't even know it was there," he said. His tone and expression seemed genuine.

He explained that other foster children also lived in the house at that time. The presence of young children meant that Jesse-Ray's foster parents were under frequent scrutiny from social workers, and if they didn't follow the letter of the law, they risked losing custody. They also might have risked being charged with child endangerment by having marijuana under their roof. So Jesse-Ray gave them a pass for snitching on him. What else could they do but name him as the user and hand the contraband over to law enforcement officers?

Jesse-Ray asserted that the true owner of the marijuana was the biological son of his foster parents. But he had no intention to snitch on him, either, having internalized the underworld code that barred sharing information with police. The boy was roughly Jesse-Ray's age, and they had been friends. He owed Jesse-Ray some pot and, too high to be sensible about it, had simply deposited it on Jesse-Ray's bed. According to Jesse-Ray's logic, the weed didn't belong to him because he had not yet taken possession of it. Thus, in his mind, he was fully and completely innocent.

Although Jesse-Ray knew who the real culprit was, he was not going to rat anyone out, especially not a good friend. After the police took him to the station, the upshot was, in Jesse-Ray's words, "I ain't going to snitch on nobody, so I took the blame."

I listened, enthralled, as Jesse-Ray told us about the interrogation. A deputy grilled him about the origin of the marijuana. I could imagine Jesse-Ray growing increasingly angry and reaching a boiling point. In his version of events, the repeated question, "Where'd it come from?" finally got on his nerves.

"I finally said, 'Fuck you. It magically appeared.'" Jesse-Ray's eyes shone as he remembered the moment. He grinned, as he always did when telling stories where he had the last word.

"We can use that [admission] in court against you," the deputy said.

Jesse-Ray responded with, "Be my guest."

Jesse-Ray wasn't as flippant with us as he had been with the deputy six months earlier. He sat in silence once Hal helped him realize that being a wanted man in the eyes of the law would hinder his future prospects. Jesse-Ray's mood darkened even further as he realized what was in store as he faced the music: the inside of a courtroom and, possibly, the inside of a jail cell.

The prospect stung even worse because he had recently taken up with a former high-school girlfriend, spending hours talking with her on the phone every night. He had become reacquainted with her online and was thrilled that she still found him attractive. A year or two earlier, she had dumped him because of his drug dealing. Now she was back in his life. He could talk of little else.

"You don't understand," he said. "I love this girl. I can't go to jail. I can't be without her."

When Monday arrived, Hal took the facts of the case to the Bluefield Union Mission, where Craig, as we'd hoped, agreed to call the court-appointed attorney. By the end of the day, everyone was on the same page: Jesse-Ray needed to turn himself in. The lawyer had counseled that timing was critical. Jesse-Ray should arrive at the police station a day and a half before the attorney's next scheduled court day representing indigent clients. That way, Jesse-Ray would end up spending only two nights in jail instead of the approximately four weeks that stood between now and that date.

As Hal had suggested might be the case, clearing up the charges would be more than just a formality but far less than a catastrophe. There was no need for Jesse-Ray to shroud himself in gloom. The attorney advised that the judge would likely sentence Jesse-Ray to time served, and Jesse-Ray would be able to walk out of court a free man.

"You see," Hal said. "You'll get this behind you and then have a clean slate."

Still, Jesse-Ray was apprehensive. He harbored fears that the judge would sentence him to months behind bars, a separation from freedom that would wreck his new romance and test his mental stability. Worse, gang norms and customs dictated against Jesse-Ray turning himself in. In the gang world, a person who turned himself in couldn't be trusted. Going through with the plan made sense in our world but might cut him off completely from his previous life.

Reluctantly, he agreed to the course of action that Hal and Craig recommended. At the same time, Jesse-Ray believed that his mental state would worsen and his recovery derail if he spent more than a couple of days in jail.

"I wouldn't be able to stand it," he said.

Hal continued to reassure him and even volunteered to drive Jesse-Ray to the police station in Marion, Virginia, to surrender, a trip that would take about an hour and a half. But central to the plan was Jesse-Ray keeping a low profile during the following month to keep him from being stopped by police in Bluefield for any reason. Engaging with police would result in him being arrested as a fugitive and shipped off to Virginia. Turning himself in closer to the court date seemed the far better option.

Sticking to the plan, Jesse-Ray carefully picked his way around Bluefield for the next month, with Hal chauffeuring him to every destination. The two of them knew that if Jesse-Ray so much as jaywalked, he could be immediately incarcerated. Nevertheless, Jesse-Ray complained that when he walked down the street, local police would ogle him.

"Of course they do!" Hal exclaimed. "Look at you!"

Hal conveyed to Jesse-Ray that his too-long saggy pants, flannel shirt, and beanie gave him the look of a ruffian. We had bought him button-down shirts and thrift-store designer pants to motivate him to wear more upscale attire, but he preferred to throw on his old clothes instead.

When the date finally arrived, Hal took advantage of the ninety-minute drive to give Jesse-Ray a motivational talk, counseling him that this situation would soon be behind him. He'd be free of any problems with law enforcement and could look ahead with no encumbrances. He could focus on furthering his education and finding a job.

But Jesse-Ray wasn't much interested in talking about progress or the future. During the month that led up to the court date, he always brought the subject back to his high school sweetheart. Most of the poetry that he emailed to me during this time sounded a single theme, trumpeting his love for her. Sadly, it wasn't his best poetry as it descended into cliché and sentimentality. But he was obsessed. Hal got the worst of it because Jesse-Ray was solely focused on his girlfriend and their relationship, and Hal allowed Jesse-Ray to dictate what they talked about, even when the themes were relentlessly self-centered.

Out of sympathy for Jesse-Ray's tender feelings for the girl, Hal left Bluefield three hours early so that the couple could meet up at a public park not far from the police station. I believed Hal's plan was overly indulgent, as once again, he was subverting his own priorities to give in to Jesse-Ray's.

Hal sat in his twenty-year-old Jeep at a discreet distance as the two of them talked and embraced. Like many young lovers, they acted like no one else in the world existed. But in this case, Jesse-

Ray acted as if *Hal* didn't exist. Jesse-Ray never even introduced his girlfriend to Hal. When Hal told me about it later, I was distressed that Jesse-Ray had been so inconsiderate, especially since Hal had given up a day of work and paid for gas to help the teenager.

"It's disrespectful," I said. But Hal was quick to excuse the behavior. He chalked it up to immaturity and his never being taught manners. Hal believed that Jesse-Ray would improve with time, and he thought that being a good role model would give Jesse-Ray better ideas about what it meant to be a man.

When he dropped Jesse-Ray off at the police station that Wednesday afternoon, Hal promised that he'd return on Friday. Ever concerned about Jesse-Ray's morale, he pointed out that this was a mere forty-eight hours, hoping that Jesse-Ray wouldn't sink into despair.

However, it was not to be. We didn't know it at the time, but a paperwork snafu had occurred.

The lawyer had promised that Jesse-Ray would call Hal on Friday afternoon to give him the word that everything had gone as planned. When the phone didn't ring, Hal feared that Jesse-Ray would be looking for him and feel betrayed by his absence. So, taking no chances, he again made the ninety-minute drive to the jail, only to be told that Jesse-Ray was at a different jail in Abingdon, Virginia, half an hour away.

At the other jail, Hal learned that not only was Jesse-Ray still locked up, but that the jail personnel adamantly refused to let Hal talk with him. Nor did they offer any reason for Jesse-Ray's continued imprisonment.

The next two days were painful for both Hal and Jesse-Ray. They had grown close as their mentor-mentee relationship deepened. Now, each was convinced that the other had walked away. The prospect of a split hurt because of their growing emotional ties. Hal was the first and last person Jesse-Ray spoke to each day. Jesse-Ray would call Hal to ask, "Dog, can I talk to you?" Hal would sit for hours listening to Jesse-Ray fret about his girlfriend, voice doubts about whether he could improve his life, and brag about past exploits. Hal mostly indulged Jesse-Ray even when Jesse-Ray was stuck in negative thought patterns and a near-obsessive fixation on keeping his girlfriend happy. They had spent hours in conversation in which Jesse-Ray confided his innermost thoughts.

Later, Jesse-Ray told me that he thought that Hal had grown disgusted by his continued problems and abandoned him at the jail. Hal believed that Jesse-Ray, resourceful as he was, had found a way out of jail and, thinking Hal had given up on him, returned to his drug-dealing milieu. Miles and worlds apart, they were both in sorrow over their supposedly lost bond.

On the weekend, Jesse-Ray was allowed a brief phone call during which he called to explain the situation and begged Hal to bail him out. "It will only cost you a hundred dollars," Jesse-Ray said. Hal urged him to sit tight and endure the weekend until things could be sorted out. Jesse-Ray's call ended abruptly, mid-sentence, as the jail set limits on phone time.

It was clear that the situation was agonizing for both men. I was starting to think that Hal had lost perspective in dealing with Jesse-Ray. He seemed blind to the excessive demands Jesse-Ray made on him. I hoped that this request for bail money and the expectation that Hal would drop everything to drive more than a hundred miles would open Hal's eyes.

I needn't have worried. As relieved as Hal was to get the call, he had no intention of putting up money when Jesse-Ray would soon be released. Plus, Hal had already spent three wasted hours on the road on Friday afternoon. Even selfless Hal was willing to set some limits!

I told Hal I was glad he drew the line. Hal assured me that he would no longer let Jesse-Ray take advantage of him or his generosity. I wondered if Hal would hold to it.

"I will," he vowed, though he admitted that he'd acted like a mother hen as he'd shepherded Jesse-Ray through the jail experience. He justified his intervention on the grounds that the wrap-up of the court case was a milestone. "He can't focus on his future and get serious about finding a job and starting school until these legal troubles are put behind him," Hal said.

It was Monday morning before Hal could reach the court-appointed attorney, who had no idea that Jesse-Ray was still in lockup. It turned out that the judge, as expected, had ordered Jesse-Ray freed. So what had happened? It took the lawyer a few minutes to get to the bottom of the situation. Court personnel had messed up the paperwork, which delayed word to the jail staff. That's why they'd put him back in lockup instead of turning him loose.

In total, Jesse-Ray spent five days in jail. As Jesse-Ray was sprung on a Monday, it was almost two weeks later before I was able to grill him about the experience. We stood in the front yard in the shade of the pine trees. The day was sunny and crisp. I stood downwind from Jesse-Ray as he chain-smoked.

At first, he refused to discuss the experience.

"Don't tell me you're quoting from the underworld rulebook again," I said.

"What happens in jail stays in jail," he declared.

I rolled my eyes. "I'm not going to reveal anyone's identity in my writing, and neither will you in your poetry."

One thing about Jesse-Ray: Once he believed his talk fell into a category different from "snitching," he'd spill. He'd tell us almost anything except the true names of people and the cities where crimes took place. The only detail he had ever held back was the whereabouts of the buried gun in the abandoned house.

He started by telling me that he became frantic, thinking that he would forget Hal's phone number. Loath to lose the lifeline to his new life, Jesse-Ray took a sharp object and carved Hal's number into the flesh of his forearm. He showed me the pink indentations that remained visible on his skin. He was telling the truth.

The initial processing at the jail consumed most of the first night as the staff completed paperwork, handed him a mattress, and walked him to his shared cell, where he entered quietly so the other inmates wouldn't wake. He slept for a few minutes, then woke up crying, staring at the ceiling, convinced he had screwed up his chance to turn his life around.

In fact, he spent a lot of time during the next day or two crying, even though he understood that showing weakness would be a poor jailhouse tactic. He knew many people who'd been to jail, including his father. And he'd already been locked up in a juvenile detention center himself. He knew a crybaby would be a target. Yet he couldn't stanch the tears.

"I woke up dreaming I was back in the safe house. And once I started crying, I couldn't stop. I realized how much I had fucked up. I broke the code, 'Never get caught. Never turn yourself in.' It's a cardinal rule. If you turn yourself in, you're going to turn somebody else in. That's what we believe. If you're willing to do that to yourself, you're willing to do that to somebody else."

He sank deeper into despair, having violated gang etiquette but having little else to fall back on. He still hadn't had time to craft a different life with enough structure to take the place of the gang. In addition, he also fretted that his time behind bars wouldn't end as soon as promised.

"I thought that because I was a fugitive, they would keep me in jail for a couple of months. I thought that I had lost everything, including my place in the safe house. I thought that Hal had given up on me," he told me.

Gradually, though, he settled into his surroundings. After all, he'd lived in southwest Virginia for years. He knew people.

In small-town Virginia, street criminals enjoyed just a few degrees of separation. At least that was Jesse-Ray's experience.

"It turns out I knew everybody in the pod except five guys," he explained with his usual knack for finding the humor in a situation. The pod held about fifty men.

Although he had a boyish face and shambling gait, Jesse-Ray was tall and possessed an intimidating presence. Nevertheless, the pod's ringleader immediately saddled Jesse-Ray with a nickname:

"Cry." Jesse-Ray began to be hectored. Everyone called Jesse-Ray by his new moniker.

For the first day or so, Jesse-Ray ignored his tormentors. But then things escalated. Inmates began to sidle up to him, giving him a passing shove.

As he talked, I envisioned sharks circling prey. Knowing Jesse-Ray's storytelling skills and street smarts, I expected him to play a trump card.

He did. He drew from the bag of skills from his previous life. Profiting from his violent past, he traded on his reputation.

He said he didn't want to do it. "Once I get into power, everything changes," he said. "I become an asshole. I feel untouchable again."

But he couldn't risk the continued harassment—he called it "punking"—that could lead to his being seriously hurt. He might even lash out in response to being taunted and get himself into deeper trouble with the law. Neither possibility appealed. So he took the ringleader aside and whispered a word that gave pause: the name Jesse-Ray was known by on the meth-infused Virginia streets. His codename.

To this day, we don't know it. He didn't volunteer it, and we didn't ask. What did it matter to us?

To be sure, Jesse-Ray had never been fearsome or famous, like Carlos the Jackal or even Heisenberg from "Breaking Bad." But in this small Virginia town, the street name was sobering enough that the ringleader immediately blanched and apologized. He even lifted his shirt to show Jesse-Ray what he assumed would be taken as a sign of solidarity: an Aryan nation tattoo. (Jesse-Ray noted the irony of the gesture; he was neither a white supremacist nor bigoted in any way.) All he was interested in was elevating his status to ensure his safety while behind bars. He wanted the punking to stop.

Sharing his street name with the ringleader of the pod worked. The teasing and harassment stopped immediately. Inmates began giving Jesse-Ray a share of their food. He shot up to the top of the jailhouse hierarchy.

I saw a new side of Jesse-Ray when he told me what happened next. I hadn't expected to hear that once Jesse-Ray became more powerful, he would turn on someone weaker.

Jesse-Ray started to take food from another inmate—a "child beater" who had the lowest status in the pod. Child abusers are loathed on the inside and, in fact, sometimes killed by other inmates. Jesse-Ray and the other men punked the child beater, which got so bad that the guards took notice. "It wasn't long before we got him transferred out of the pod."

He nodded in satisfaction, showing no remorse.

This was a moment when I kept my expression neutral, a study in nonjudgment. I was taken aback by Jesse-Ray's easy slide from tormented to tormentor, but I wasn't sure whether or how to ask him about it. I guess I'd thought that Jesse-Ray might decline to bully someone the way he'd been bullied, regardless of the man's crime.

We moved on to another notable event during his incarceration. A man he'd known on the outside offered him drugs.

"He was old, about fifty," Jesse-Ray explained. "He had meth-mouth, bad."

I ignored the fact that Jesse-Ray dismissed someone a good ten years younger than me and Hal as "old."

"Go on," I said.

After the old man offered drugs, Jesse-Ray asked him to show what he had.

"That's the etiquette. If you say you've got some, you gotta line it out!" Jesse-Ray declared, animated.

No longer holding back, Jesse-Ray had warmed up to the jailhouse saga. In contrast to when we discussed his childhood, he seemed to enjoy my probing for particulars. He lit another cigarette, making me wait to learn whether he'd refused the drugs and, if so, what excuse he'd offered for declining to partake.

Jesse-Ray puffed, then grinned. "He didn't know I was clean

and sober," he continued. "I wasn't about to tell him. I just said, 'No, dude, not right now.'"

Jesse-Ray paused for emphasis. He shuffled his feet and took another puff of his cigarette. He looked up through the pine needles to the sky, where white clouds billowed. He had stayed clean in jail. He saw that as a triumph.

I congratulated him, then asked, "Any regrets?"

He confessed he had felt a momentary pang about disclosing his street identity to the inmates. But he quickly got over it.

He also explained that he had lost his temper once. There was one moment, when he realized that he wasn't getting out of jail on that Friday night, that could have gone south. He shouted, insisting to the jail staff that the judge had set him free. He was supposed to be out. He grabbed a piece of furniture and began to shake it. Apparently, several prison guards mobilized to ensure that he returned to his cell peacefully. Jesse-Ray had no choice but to resign himself to the confinement that would last at least another two days. The rest of the weekend passed without incident, he said.

As for Jesse-Ray's release, I had already heard that side of the story from Hal. After the attorney straightened out the paperwork, Hal had driven the Jeep to Virginia and picked up Jesse-Ray. Mentor and mentee were happy to learn that neither one had abandoned the other, as both had feared. The ordeal was over. Jesse-Ray was right with the law again.

Jesse-Ray was right about one other thing as well, as the incident with the child beater attested. Power changed him. He'd enjoyed wielding power when the inmates stopped calling him Cry. But it wasn't the anecdote about the child-beater that stuck in my mind.

After Jesse-Ray had recalled his experience of jail, he held out his wrists, one crossed over the other, to show me how his hands had been handcuffed.

"You learn to compensate, to scratch your nose or to light a cigarette one-handed," he explained, pantomiming how he'd lit a cigarette with his manacled hands. "For days after I got out, I'd talk to people, down at the mission or wherever, with one wrist crossed over the other," Jesse-Ray told me. "As if the cuffs were still on."

The words hung in the air.

Our conversation was interrupted when Hal came around the corner, calling for Jesse-Ray to help him carry some construction materials to the backyard shed. Jesse-Ray hopped to it, but I stood rooted in place, having found the moment breathtaking. To me the metaphor was obvious. But I wondered if Jesse-Ray had absorbed its meaning. Even after the handcuffs had been removed, he'd acted as if his hands were still fixed together. His mind and body hadn't caught up with the reality of his freedom.

In my opinion, he seemed stuck in a place of little forward momentum. He was happy to accept Hal's helpfully hovering presence but unwilling to declare his own goals or behave in ways that showed a new maturity.

"I'm doubtful on school," he'd told me before he'd gone to jail, even though he and Hal had already looked into the possibility of community college.

If he continued to wallow in the comfort of his old habits and balked at adopting new behaviors and ways of thinking, hadn't he simply shed his handcuffs only to willingly accept a mental straitjacket?

Though Jesse-Ray was out from behind bars, I wondered when he would truly be free.

Homeless teens often end up in jail

Jesse-Ray Lewis was not alone as a homeless teen. He was one of 35,000 "unaccompanied youth younger than 24" in the United States in 2016. Like Jesse-Ray Lewis, many homeless young people sleep in abandoned buildings. They also occupy park benches and makeshift shelters or stay with strangers.

Jesse-Ray Lewis was also among the 44 percent of homeless youth who reported a stay in jail, prison, or a detention center in 2016.

"Far too many young people will come into contact with the justice system as a result of their lack of safe and stable housing," says Naomi Smoot, executive director of the Coalition for Juvenile Justice.

Not only are unstable living arrangements a problem, but homeless young people may also "engage in behavior to survive that can lead to arrests," writes Jennifer Pokempner, child welfare policy director of the Juvenile Law Center.

Many young people remain locked up because they don't have a home to go back to. Even if they are old enough to live on their own, they have no money to pay for an apartment or other lodging.

The National Council for Juvenile and Family Court Judges authored a resolution in the summer of 2017 that "opposes the criminalization of youth" when their behavior stems from being homeless. The resolution also acknowledges a role for judges in identifying young people "who are at risk of homelessness and proactively addressing their needs through planning and connection with resources."

Experts say that judges play a key role, even if they don't realize the potential of their effect on youth.

"What happens in the legal system often makes the difference between whether their next stop after the courtroom is a home, a shelter, or under a bridge," says Casey Trupin, program officer of youth homelessness for the Raikes Foundation. "What judges do, inside and outside of their courtroom, can change . . . the courts-to-streets pipeline."

A federal framework to end homelessness by 2020 calls for better data collection and more coordination among state, local, and federal systems, and for the development of a model to create interventions that work.

CHAPTER 5

Nightmares and the death of grandma

I want to fast forward a couple of years
my tears of sadness and depression gone.

From stressful
to successful.

Pondering the thought
of being taught nothing
that I had no reason for living.

—Jesse-Ray Lewis,
"Anticipation from Another State"

After a couple of months in the safe house, Jesse-Ray seemed sleep deprived. He looked haggard and worn, with dark bags under his eyes. He couldn't seem to stifle his yawns. Hal had trouble rousing him for his volunteer shifts at the Bluefield Union Mission, relating that even though he called him on the phone every morning, it took many minutes for Jesse-Ray to answer, even though the sun was up long before his alarm rang at 8 a.m. Sometimes Jesse-Ray hit the snooze button and stayed in bed, and Hal was forced to walk next door and rap loudly on the door to wake him.

We soon found out the reason. Jesse-Ray confided in Hal, admitting that vivid, terrifying nightmares were interrupting his sleep. He'd sit straight up in bed, filled with horror, unable to relax until early morning. Then, toward dawn, he'd fall back to sleep, going into an especially deep state just as Hal tried to rouse him.

Were the dreams related to drug withdrawal? Flashbacks? Hallucinations? Jesse-Ray said that doctors had examined him after the Commonwealth of Virginia put him into foster care and, later, juvenile detention. These doctors had told him that he suffered from post-traumatic stress disorder, or PTSD—the result of the things he'd seen, heard, and experienced, including physical abuse and the death of his cousin Zach.

The worst parts of Jesse-Ray's childhood seemed to be related to his father, which triggered Hal's sympathy. Hal was convinced that if he could be a positive male role model for Jesse-Ray, the teenager could rise above his damaging childhood.

Hal spent time with Jesse-Ray every day, hearing many of Jesse-Ray's stories. To give Jesse-Ray a change of scene, he'd take him along on errands. If Jesse-Ray wanted to spend his food-stamp money at Walmart, Hal would drive him the three miles to the store rather than expect him to take the bus. In addition, they had heart-to-heart talks every night after Jesse-Ray's Narcotics Anonymous meeting. If the memories became uncomfortable and Jesse-Ray wanted to change the subject, Hal would let him. Hal never asked tough questions the way I did, poking ever deeper into the layers of trauma that made up Jesse-Ray's past.

I suspected that my interviews with Jesse-Ray might be a likely cause of the night terrors. When Jesse-Ray discussed his memories with me on the weekends, our talks sometimes lasted for hours. We would focus on one incident until I felt I understood it from all angles. The subject matter was melodramatic, sensational, and horrifying, touching on his victimization though abuse and rape. Though he suffered as he relived these experiences, I felt stirrings of excitement because I knew his poems were powerful, raw, and affecting. I was convinced that Jesse-Ray's perceptiveness coupled with his struggles could produce a literary experience that would touch hearts and maybe change lives. I hoped Jesse-Ray would come to believe in his own potential, possibly even pursue a writing career. Given to sassy language and morbid metaphors, he was a fresh talent, and as a former journalist, I could not resist the temptation to draw the details of his life from him.

Cementing my image of Jesse-Ray as an artist-in-the-making was his childhood habit of keeping journals. He told me that, as early as he could remember, writing had become an outlet, a way to launch himself out of his war-zone of worries into a world of words. He grew animated when he talked about his favorite book, *Crank*, Ellen Hopkins' epic novel-in-poems about her daughter's life in the grip of the monster of drug abuse. He had come upon it sometime during high school, and the book had made a lasting impression.

Because Jesse-Ray had discovered catharsis through the process of writing his childhood diaries, it was easy for me to rationalize and justify the way I was dragging him through painful territory. The nightmares, however, gave me pause and forced me to question my judgment. In some ways I felt culpable. How could our conversations not have provoked nightmares?

The memory of his grandmother was Exhibit A. I pictured a weather-beaten, gray-haired woman in a housecoat. Jesse-Ray said no. He remembered Mom, as he called her, as youngish and nice looking.

The adults in Jesse-Ray's home were always stoned, and his grandmother was no exception. In fact, Jesse-Ray said that the only adult in a sober frame of mind ever to set foot in the house was a child-protection worker once sent to do a home visit by the state.

In this unlovely scenario, his grandmother was a hardcore drug user. A friend of hers was a frequent supplier. The friend would stop by to bring Mom pills or weed or some harder drug, and before long everyone would be bombed.

They lived in squalor. According to Jesse-Ray, Mom never went anywhere. Jesse-Ray's father dominated the two of them, taking care of any practical matters that involved leaving the house. "I don't remember her leaving . . . *ever*," Jesse-Ray said.

When Mom talked to Jesse-Ray, she treated him like a confidant. She told him about the miseries of her upbringing including her own childhood rape and how her mother had refused to believe her.

He learned other pieces of questionable family lore from Mom, such as when he was first served "bitter potatoes" when he was just three years old. He didn't remember anyone ever cooking a meal for him—not even Mom. But he remembered the dish involving mashed potatoes mixed with Xanax. Mom told him he had liked it and ate up every spoonful, even as a toddler.

No wonder he was stoned most days at school. Xanax was only a part of the panoply of drugs and alcohol that shaped his waking moments.

Mom also related violent incidents from his childhood, such as his father insisting that men and boys don't cry. She said that when Jesse-Ray cried, his father would slap him to make him stop.

Despite Mom's obvious lack of parenting (or grandparenting) skills, Jesse-Ray loved her dearly. He said she was virtually the only person who was kind to him during his childhood. She was a source of both stability and solidarity.

He grew accustomed to the idea of family as defined by his father's and grandmother's world views. He accepted his place.

"Where I'm from, you're never a kid," he explained. "If you can walk and talk, you're not a kid. You should be able to hear things and see things and do things just like everybody else." That included hearing about Mom's childhood rape. Jesse-Ray seemed puzzled by my reaction that her trauma wasn't a fit subject for discussion with a child. To him, his grandmother's revelation wasn't odd. Rather, it was simply part of the fabric of his life, in which the adults never allowed the presence of a child to temper their pronouncements. He was neutral about what had happened to her, as he was detached about most everything in his childhood.

Mom never spoke unless she was alone with Jesse-Ray. Only when she was in a room with him would she find her voice. That circumstance rarely arose "because there were always people in the house doing shit," Jesse-Ray explained. He remembered her as either silent or sharing almost unfathomable confidences.

What did she discuss during those rare interludes of solitude with her grandson?

"She would talk about how fucked up everything was in the world," he said. "How you never could trust people. She would say, 'Even your family can fuck you in the ass and not even give you a reach-around.'"

Jesse-Ray gave one of his trademark grins and chuckled at the memory of her phrasing. I didn't know exactly what the idiom meant, but I'd gotten the gist of it. As we moved on, I tried to draw feelings out of Jesse-Ray, even though it was something he rarely discussed. I wondered about the emotional quality of his memory of his grandmother. His picture of her was indelible and positive, despite the fact that she had used him as a sounding board for her own despair when he was only a child.

On those cold nights when she told him to imagine *Little House on the Prairie*, for instance, she might as well have been referring to a volcano in Hawaii or to a cavern on Venus because he had no frame of reference. And yet, the sound of her voice and the magic of her words lulled him to sleep. Sometimes she would sing to him. "She was just a really kind person," he said.

After Jesse-Ray finished describing his grandmother's life, it was time to talk about her death. Dislodging Jesse-Ray's memories of that night was like watching glass shatter.

Before I took him back through that night for a minute-by-minute recounting, I already knew that Mom had died in his arms. He had disclosed that fact, without embellishment, shortly after we met him. But in this more detailed account, he gave up a new, significant fact: Jesse-Ray felt in part that he had caused her death, even though he was only eleven or twelve years old at the time.

The day it happened, Jesse-Ray had been badgering Mom, but

he no longer remembered what about. They had argued. He had persisted. Her response had burned into his memory. In the midst of their argument, she cried out, "You're going to give me a heart attack!"

Later that night, Mom's drug-supplying friend woke him from the couch where he'd fallen asleep. "She fell!" the woman had cried.

He ran through the tiny doorway into the kitchen, past the black mini-fridge, and into the living room that doubled as a bedroom, complete with mattress on the floor and old box TV. He saw immediately that she was dying, if not already dead. Jesse-Ray pulled her head into his lap, telling her repeatedly that he loved her. Foam seeped from her lips, and he wiped it away, touching her eyelids with butterfly-soft fingers, closing her eyes. He put off calling the paramedics so that he could relish the physicality of her, the smell of her, the cradling of her. He did not want to let her go.

"I still wake up thinking I am hugging Momma," he wrote in a poem. "When she died, that's when my life became hell."

Not even in his teens, Jesse-Ray had lost his protector. His beloved Mom was gone. No one was left to buffer him against the callousness and indifference of his father.

The evidence was clear to the visiting child protection service worker—the one sober adult who ever entered the house, as Jesse-Ray remembered it. The social worker saw drug paraphernalia clearly visible around the residence with no attempt made to hide it. Between the prospect of foster care and the custody of his father, the state ultimately deemed the father the greater of two evils.

With Mom gone, Jesse-Ray entered the world of foster care.

How much of this was true? Hal and I were occasionally forced to ask ourselves this question as we tried to put together the puzzle of his life and figure out how we could help. Our hearts went out to him as we learned more about his past. We were touched by an email he sent to me: "I can't wait to have a mind absent of fear, hate, anger, and sadness. I just want peace. For once in my life I have people that I want to be like."

We located documents that outlined his time in foster care. The fact that he spent years as a ward of the state was beyond dispute. Other acts of violence he described were not easy to verify, such as the cruelty of his dad toward him. But I had no doubt the story of his grandmother's death was true. And shortly after that conversation, the safe house became a place of nightmares, at least from midnight to dawn. Jesse-Ray was haggard when morning came, sometimes still shaking with fear, which elicited even more maternal, protective feelings from Hal.

In one nightmare that Jesse-Ray described, Mom was sitting right in front of him, in a chair. She spoke accusingly and glared at him. He said he experienced it like real life. He felt it was happening. The apparition was angry and blamed him for her death. She'd said he would give her a heart attack, and she'd been right.

When he woke, he couldn't believe the psychic visitation was just a dream. He wondered if he was losing his mind. Shortly thereafter, Jesse-Ray wrote a poignant poem that ended with the phrase, "I hope someone will forgive me for what I've done."

When I came home the next weekend, he told me, eyes narrowed, "I can't talk about her anymore."

Easy come, easy go

Why is it that some addicts make friends easily but never commit to any one person or place for long? Could it be related to neural wiring constructed in the brain during childhood?

Some researchers suggest that addictions derive from a child's insecure attachment to his or her caregiver. If a child fails to receive the love and care he or she deserves, drugs or the thrill of risky behavior can become a balm for emotional distress.

In fact, the success of twelve-step groups may come because they provide a "surrogate attachment," a way for the addict to eschew isolation and learn to take chances, within a supportive environment, by emotionally connecting with others.

The lifelong repercussions that childhood trauma can cause are shockingly high. In a major study, researchers identified "Adverse Childhood Experiences" or ACE. In twenty years of research on 17,421 people, they traced two-thirds of all alcoholism to ACE. Further, they linked half of all drug abuse and three quarters of all intravenous drug use to ACE. The ACE Study began in 1995 at Kaiser Permanente in conjunction with the US government Centers for Disease Control and Prevention.

A person's childhood traumas—or ACE, as the researchers called them—aren't typically on display. The passage of time may obscure them, shame may push them underground, and social taboo may shroud them.

The late Swiss psychoanalyst Alice Miller, author of noted books on child abuse, states that a person's body stores up the truth about his or her childhood, "and although we can repress it, we can never alter it. Our intellect can be deceived, our feelings manipulated, our conceptions confused, and our body tricked with medication. But someday our body will present its bill, for it is as incorruptible as a child, who, still whole in spirit, will accept no compromises or excuses, and it will not stop tormenting us until we stop evading the truth."

Miller wrote that coerced, physically punished, or abused children carry mental illness and insecurity through life. They often cycle the abuse to the next generation and sometimes, in a perverse desire to distinguish themselves, achieve monumental things. They sometimes work feverishly to reach the pinnacles of their professions.

All of this adds up to an "attachment disorder" in the minds of psychiatrists like Miller. But the strong diagnostic label may be too heavy for many families to stomach, even as they witness their addicted loved one make friends easily, exhibiting almost effortless charisma. Before long, those friendships predictably go to ashes. How many times have you heard an alcoholic or addict euphemistically called "a drifter"?

Even some trained professionals argue that an "attachment disorder" may not describe every alcoholic or drug addict. Because people who turn to drink or drugs have a tough time dealing with their feelings, especially uncomfortable ones, "emotional immaturity" is a description that might be more accurate and easier for families to accept. Rehab experts argue that addicts must work to develop "emotional sobriety" before their recovery can be complete. Otherwise they may have given up alcohol and drugs only to become so-called "dry drunks," viewing their life in recovery as a prison sentence.

With Jesse-Ray, we may have experienced a dry-drunk moment when, after a few weeks of Narcotics Anonymous meetings, he seemed miffed, arguing that Hal and I needed to trust him. He complained that in being asked to follow rules, he felt like he was "on probation."

People who are not emotionally mature struggle to develop meaningful relationships. They may be either too needy or overbearing. A pessimistic outlook may cast a shadow on their lives as they face a future that appears to be threatening or hostile. Low self-esteem is a curse keeping them from believing that they deserve more in life.

A symptom seen in people with emotional immaturity is one that we often saw in Jesse-Ray: They seemingly can't live in the present moment but spend their time ruminating about the past or worrying about the future. Jesse-Ray fretted constantly about the prospect that he might be kicked out of the safe house.

An alcoholic or drug addict may be charismatic and able to win people over with their personal magnetism. They may seem adept at using people to meet their needs. Underneath the charm may be the desire to manipulate or an inability to commit. According to addiction expert Alice M. Lebron, "Alcoholics/addicts appear to have a sixth sense in identifying vulnerabilities . . . appearing to offer caring and concern if it might help them develop a relationship to meet their needs."

CHAPTER 6

Fathers and father figures

I remember being
on the playground
thinking, damn
if I jumped off this slide
I could go home
sneak into my dad's room
and take some of them candies
that made me feel silly.

Once, I ate seven and felt like
I was going to heaven.
I was seven years old.

Didn't know what they were
until my dad caught me
and taught me how to snort them properly.

—Jesse-Ray Lewis, "Seven and Seven"

Once, right after preparing a meal for Jesse-Ray and eating together at our dining room table, Hal and I fell into an impromptu game using our safari-animal-shaped napkin rings as toys. We hopped the wooden animals around on the tabletop, making them bound and play, clowning on Jesse-Ray's behalf. We were trying to show him that relationships don't have to be heavy—they could be playful and light. We offered him a lion-shaped napkin ring so he could join the play, but he backed away. "Y'all are crazy," he said, managing a grin but unable to relax and enjoy the simple camaraderie.

Shortly after we met, Jesse-Ray once told me that he feared getting close to people because he knew it wouldn't end well. He hated the thought of hurting anyone. I remember thinking that Jesse-Ray was probably talking about Hal, knowing somehow in advance that he would let Hal down.

Long before Jesse-Ray had appeared on the scene, Hal had dedicated himself to the renovation of the safe house. The roof had leaked, the wiring needed repair and replacing, and the floors reeked of cooped-up animals. When Hal completed the first stage of renovations, those same animals could have eaten off those scrubbed floors. Everyone who'd seen the inside had exclaimed over the hardwood floors, the pristine shower, and the windows adjoining the porch covered with decorative planks of wood, which he'd hand-painted with a deep red-and-black finish.

The countertops gleamed. Walls were patched and painted. Trim was polished. Rebuilt radiators were strategically placed. The whole living space sparkled with Hal's workmanship. Architectural details restored a sense of things being plumb in the crooked, hundred-year-old house. If it had been marketed as a bed-and-breakfast suite, many people might have responded to its charms.

This cozy picture was turned upside down after Jesse-Ray had been there for three months.

I was at work the day Hal discovered how filthy Jesse-Ray had been keeping the safe house. That unwelcome intelligence came as a shock, because cleaning up after himself was one of Jesse-Ray's few obligations. How hard could it be to sweep up and keep the counters clean?

The jolt was a seismic one for Hal, because he had poured so much time and effort into Jesse-Ray, believing that the teen would not only survive but also flourish under his care and attention. Hal had been relentlessly positive, a cheerleader in Jesse-Ray's corner. He urged Jesse-Ray to believe in himself, keep his spirits high and work hard to take advantage of the free food and shelter the Bluefield Union Mission was providing. He pointed out that, thanks to the mission, Jesse-Ray had the chance to chart his future without having to worry about the daily practicalities of paying for food and accommodation.

Hal was motivated by his personal experience of being sent to live in Miami when he was seventeen years old. When he was Jesse-Ray's age, he'd had a deep yearning for a helping hand, believing that a male guardian figure might have kept him out of trouble and made his life easier. Instead, he had been forced to figure things out on his own, and some of the lessons had been painful. So he expected his influence to produce good things when it came to Jesse-Ray.

Every Tuesday morning, Hal made sure Jesse-Ray carried the garbage outside, which often involved rousing a reluctant Jesse-Ray first by phone and then knocking loudly on the door. Jesse-Ray never could seem to get the hang of an alarm clock. Out of respect for Jesse-Ray's privacy, Hal hadn't stepped foot inside the place since the young man moved in. Further, he'd been careful not to issue too many demands, knowing that Jesse-Ray had resented his overbearing father. Hal simply reminded Jesse-Ray every day to keep the place clean, thinking this would be enough to ensure compliance.

Hal had never wanted to police anyone's clean-up efforts. However, his simple reminders had turned out to be less than effective, and Jesse-Ray had done as he pleased.

On that Tuesday morning, Hal phoned Jesse-Ray, but Jesse-Ray didn't pick up. Hal thumped on the back door, but no amount of banging seemed to rouse the teenager. Frustrated, Hal punched in the keypad code and went inside to wake Jesse-Ray. He was shocked by the state of the safe house.

"Jesse-Ray!" Hal hollered from the kitchen. "Are you awake? This place stinks!"

"What's up?" Jesse-Ray called groggily from his bedroom. "Sorry, man. I woke up, but I fell back to sleep."

Hal walked through the L-shaped interior that led from the kitchen to the living room to the bedroom. Jesse-Ray was just getting out of bed.

"I thought we had an agreement," Hal said, growing more upset. "You were supposed to clean up every day. You obviously haven't been doing it. This place is too far gone."

"Oh, I meant to clean up when I got home, but at the end of the day I was tired. And then I always wake up in the middle of the night and can't sleep, so I'm tired in the mornings, too."

Jesse-Ray's excuses intensified Hal's annoyance. "If you're awake in the middle of the night, then that's when you should be cleaning up!"

As Jesse-Ray pulled clothes from the mounds of piled-up jeans and shirts that were strewn around the bedroom, Hal began a closer inspection of the safe house. He had noticed that Jesse-Ray hadn't disposed of crumbs or food packaging in the kitchen. There was a two-inch space between the floor and the bottom of the lowest kitchen shelves, and Jesse-Ray had simply kicked the dirt and crumbs and wrappers beneath the shelves. Ants marched along the kitchen counters and across the vinyl floor, where they swarmed over the computer desk. Food remnants and wrappers were in evidence there as well.

With Hal's discovery of each new transgression, Jesse-Ray was treated to an earful.

"Look at these ants! You've been having your food over at the desk after I told you numerous times, 'No eating at the computer!'"

"Hey, man, I thought I was keepin' it clean," Jesse-Ray protested.

"This isn't anywhere near clean!" Hal fumed. "I can't believe you disrespected me and my place. I told you not to leave food out. Why can't you put it in the trash?"

Hal moved into the bathroom. It was worse.

"There's pee all over the floor and the walls!" Hal was incredulous.

By this time, Jesse-Ray was fully dressed, though his light-brown curls were still tousled.

"Well, I didn't do it on purpose," he managed to reply.

"I don't want to hear any more excuses."

"Well, no one ever showed me how to clean."

Hal, his anger rising, couldn't resist sarcasm. "I suppose no one told you how to separate clean clothes from dirty clothes either?"

Jesse-Ray had an answer to everything. "We never had dressers, so our things were all over the place."

"That explains the clothes. But everyone knows you're supposed to piss in the toilet. Why is there pee on the floor and the walls?"

"I don't see too well when I first get up."

"If you can't hit the toilet when you're standing, sit down on the seat."

"Are you mad at me?" Jesse-Ray asked, almost in surprise.

Hal stood still for a moment to reflect. He knew that Jesse-Ray's father had never reasoned with him and, if Jesse-Ray's version of his childhood was true, his father had been brutal in forcing his son to do his bidding. Hal chose his words carefully.

"I'm not angry. I'm disappointed. I treated you nicely, and this is how you paid me back. You didn't even bother to keep my place decent."

Jesse-Ray had no comeback because the evidence was clear. However, he did offer the feeble excuse that his grandmother's house had been a place of squalor, and messiness was a familiar state.

Hal snorted in response. Then he made a quick decision. No longer was he going to tiptoe around Jesse-Ray's sensitive feelings. Even though he wanted to shield Jesse-Ray from the worst of his wrath, Hal was peeved enough to stop sugar-coating reality. Because Jesse-Ray was a chain-smoker, Hal had always made sure Jesse-

Ray didn't run out of cigarettes, even if he occasionally had to front Jesse-Ray the money to buy them. Jesse-Ray already grappled with cold-turkey sobriety, and it seemed unfair to expect him to give up smoking at the same time. Nevertheless, Hal told Jesse-Ray, "No more cigarettes until I see this place clean."

Hal stood and surveyed the interior of the safe house from the living room. He knew a day of clean-up would be required to make the place habitable again. The sad fact was that Jesse-Ray knew no more about how to clean and put things in order than our border collie, Sadie, knew how to do advanced calculus.

"You've trashed this apartment," Hal said. "You said you don't know how to do housekeeping. If that's true, then I'll show you." He knew that Jesse-Ray, big and lumbering, would likely get in the way and slow things down. But Hal resolved to summon patience and teach Jesse-Ray a few simple housekeeping techniques.

The stench was so bad that Hal wore a mask. Dirt, food, food wrappers, cigarette butts, gum, loose tobacco, and indeterminate objects littered the sticky floors. The countertops were gummed up. Foul-smelling clothes had to be fished out of the piles where they were lumped with clean ones. Hal launched into tidying-up with vigor, noticing Jesse-Ray's clumsy efforts out of the corner of his eye every now and then.

"That's not the way to sweep!" he exclaimed, losing his patience. "Gimme that broom!"

He set Jesse-Ray to scrubbing the bathroom walls. When he realized the teenager's ineffectual swipes weren't accomplishing much, Hal pushed him aside and attacked the urine-spotted walls with bleach and elbow grease.

About three hours into the cleanup, Hal spied Jesse-Ray sitting down doing nothing. Hal erupted.

"Why am I here busting my butt when I'm a sixty-five-year-old man and you're a teenager! Get up and get moving!"

Hal told me about the mess during our phone conversation at the end of the day. He also told me about the crackdown. He portrayed himself as tough, recounting how he'd warned Jesse-Ray that he was going to get himself thrown out of the safe house if he kept this up.

But I knew Hal as a softie, and I suspected his resolve might be short-lived, even though he was hopping mad.

"Are you sure you won't start coddling Jesse-Ray again?" I asked skeptically. "You've always cut him slack and made excuses for his bad behavior."

For example, Hal had told Jesse-Ray that he could have the compact refrigerator that sat on the back porch since we'd upgraded to a larger refrigerator for my studio apartment in Blacksburg. Craig hadn't wanted a refrigerator or stove in the safe house because the Bluefield Union Mission would be providing the lodgers' food. But Hal thought Jesse-Ray might like to have the small fridge for his sodas and leftovers. The fridge sat outside for a couple of weeks until Hal eventually scrubbed it and set it up in the kitchen. He had rewarded Jesse-Ray's laziness by doing the chore for him.

And, if it so much as drizzled, Hal would spare Jesse-Ray the five-minute walk to the Bluefield Union Mission for his work shift. "I can't believe you're driving him," I'd exclaim. "Let him walk! A few raindrops aren't going to hurt him. He's not going to melt!" There were staff members at the Bluefield Union Mission who lived farther away but still walked there every day, rain or shine.

I might have been less inclined than Hal to put up with Jesse-Ray's lack of effort because Jesse-Ray had been saying things that gave me pause. He'd declare his life drug-free, claiming, "That's the past. It's done and over with." Then, in the next breath, he'd express that once he had gotten a job and his own place, he would smoke pot to ease his mind.

After he got out of jail, he'd told me, "I feel like I have this overwhelming pressure to succeed, and it makes me doubt everything." I didn't see any point in stepping in to do Jesse-Ray's work for him if he wasn't fully committed and willing to exert himself.

I thought my view was more realistic than Hal's, and I accused him of taking Jesse-Ray's declarations of willingness to do his part at face value, even when it was obvious that Jesse-Ray's efforts were faltering and lame. "I'm done with that," Hal stated flatly, referring to his tendency to appease, humor, and dote on Jesse-Ray. "It's a new day." I only half-believed him.

And what of housekeeping? Again, I suspected that, even after Hal's dramatic sanitizing intervention, Jesse-Ray wouldn't know how to respond to the overly general command, "Keep the house clean." I suggested to Hal that he break the tasks down into steps and post them in the safe house kitchen.

Hal did so, posting half a dozen rules in the kitchen of the safe house. When I came home for the weekend, Hal showed me a copy of the list:

- No food on computer desk!
- Empty garbage every day!
- Wash all utensils and dishes after each meal!
- Sweep up all food and crumbs after each meal!

And so forth.

I praised Hal, who was happy that I approved, especially since I'd criticized him for being too lenient.

In retrospect, Hal realized that he should have exercised greater oversight from the start. He should have made clear how vital it was that Jesse-Ray not fail to keep the safe house clean. Hal should have insisted on making at least weekly inspections. And he should have introduced consequences, such as refusing to do things or buy things for Jesse-Ray before Jesse-Ray had completed his chores. Even after he discovered that Jesse-Ray had been living in filth, Hal didn't alert Craig at the Bluefield Union Mission to Jesse-Ray's slovenly living conditions, which in turn might have triggered additional consequences or warnings. Hal couldn't stop himself from being overly protective.

However, I also understood that Hal had been treating Jesse-Ray with kid gloves because of what Jesse-Ray had told us about his upbringing. Hal wanted to provide the biggest contrast possible between himself and Jesse-Ray's father.

Jesse-Ray's memories were of a brutish and unloving man. He had told Hal that his father had been in the military and related to his son like a drill sergeant.

"He was always being bossed around and told what to do," Hal told me. "There was always verbal harassment and belittling. He was always being beaten when he was younger. Nothing he did was right."

Hal suspected that Jesse-Ray would react badly to a male presence that was too authoritarian. He believed that Jesse-Ray had been deprived of a good male role model, which many people take for granted. He was determined to help Jesse-Ray set an upward trajectory for his life, so he sought to maintain Jesse-Ray's confidence and rapport. Hal believed that if he maintained a consistently kind demeanor, it would provide a sharp contrast with the fear-inspiring tenor of Jesse-Ray's childhood home. As a result, even after the cleaning frenzy, Hal continued to be a cordial, gracious, and gentle influence, trying to teach Jesse-Ray by example, tiptoeing around Jesse-Ray's feelings, and issuing few demands.

Whenever Jesse-Ray boasted of achieving some small accomplishment such as getting to work on time or studying math to meet the community college entrance requirement, Hal would say, "I'm proud of you!"

The first time he made this declaration was after the two of them had visited Bluefield State College, a West Virginia state university situated within walking distance of our home, where Jesse-Ray had patiently filled out several applications and financial aid forms.

"What?" he asked quizzically, as if the compliment hadn't registered. He gave Hal a sidelong glance. Jesse-Ray would study us out of the corners of his eyes when we said things that puzzled or astounded him, which was often. "No one's ever said that to me before."

Responses like that from Jesse-Ray convinced Hal that his low-key, benevolent approach was working. When Jesse-Ray, on his own, halved his cigarette smoking to ten a day, or when he reported to Hal that he believed college was a desirable goal, Hal would say, "I'm proud of you!" He couldn't repeat it enough.

"When I counseled Jesse-Ray to become more organized or to take on more responsibility, I approached it from an educational way rather than a militaristic way," Hal later explained to me. "Jesse-Ray never had a mother or father figure that took an interest in him. There was a spiritual aspect to my coaching him in a loving way and showing him about responsibility rather than just making demands."

Sometimes Jesse-Ray would ask Hal how he could repay the Bluefield Union Mission and Hal for all they were providing.

"I explained that he didn't have to have money to repay everything," Hal said. "I told him that living up to his responsibilities, including keeping the place clean, was the best way to pay us all back. In hindsight, I should have checked up on what Jesse-Ray was doing in the safe house. But I was hoping my words would be enough."

In my opinion, Hal allowed the harrowing facts of Jesse-Ray's childhood to cloud his judgment, which resulted in his reticence to intervene instead of enforcing standards of cleanliness. Hal had meticulously renovated the property, and his hands-off approach to its maintenance was out of character, knowing how quickly tenants could trash a place. (He had owned and renovated rental homes in Florida and was an experienced landlord.) But with Jesse-Ray, Hal's lax oversight stemmed from his trouble finding the balance between issuing commands and setting basic housekeeping expectations.

While I was removed from the day-to-day of Jesse-Ray's life

in Bluefield, I was struck by the dark and despairing tenor of the writing that Jesse-Ray emailed to me, some of it prompted by memories of his father. Most of his writing depicted misery, such as when he referred to the "drowning body of thoughts buried deep inside, ones I try to hide." As I read these expressions of agony, depression, and sadness, I understood Hal's instinct to be gentle with Jesse-Ray. He had been born a drug baby, had graduated barely literate from high school, had fallen into employment with a meth-dealing gang, and had suffered a winter of homelessness. It was a wonder he'd survived. But unlike Hal, I didn't let my sympathies get in the way of my actions. I pushed Jesse-Ray to improve his writing and to broaden his literary range.

"How about expressing wonder or delight?" I once asked him. "How about writing about something to be celebrated?"

He shook his head as if he didn't understand the concept.

When I asked if he could summon up a pleasant memory from his childhood, he maintained that he could not name a single one. He told us that as he grew older, he developed a camaraderie of sorts with his father based on mutual insults.

"He always said, 'I am going to be extra hard on you because you are my son,'" Jesse-Ray told me. "If my father was on his deathbed, I'd probably insult him. I would probably get mad at him for dying."

He recounted how he would get into physical fights with his dad. They'd beat each other, sometimes until one or the other was knocked out cold.

"More than once I thought he'd killed me or that I'd killed him," he said.

"That doesn't make sense. How did you know if you were the one killed?" I asked.

Jesse-Ray flashed a smile, and the corners of his eyes crinkled as he gave a little laugh. "When I woke up three days later."

I asked what would start the fights.

"Anything," Jesse-Ray said. As he got older, he'd provoke his dad. Then the fight would begin, with one of them ending up on the ground, semi-comatose.

We didn't know how much of this was true. Hal would occasionally stop by the Bluefield Union Mission to chat with the staff when he'd drop Jesse-Ray off or stop by to make a donation of used clothes or goods. Jesse-Ray rubbed shoulders with at least a half dozen staff members or volunteers during the day as he performed tasks including lifting crates at the loading dock, breaking down cardboard boxes, or straightening up displays in the thrift store. One day, Hal heard from a staff member that Jesse-Ray had told everyone that his dad used to hit him with a baseball bat to make him go to sleep. None of them believed it, the staff member said.

Garrulous with his Bluefield Union Mission co-workers, Jesse-Ray also freely offered up details and descriptions of his childhood during his weekend conversations with me. Our talks opened my eyes to an existence I could hardly fathom. Reading the lines of verse he sent me often felt like a punch in the gut. He wrote convincingly of ice, flames, barbed wire, and his scorched heart.

Two trap houses and two men were central to Jesse-Ray's life and writing—his father and a man he called Rick.

Jesse-Ray learned the big-time meth trade from Rick, which was not his real name. Rick ran trap houses. But unlike the trap house where Jesse-Ray grew up, Rick kept his houses pristine and spare. Footprints and tire ruts from customers would not be tolerated, much less the accoutrements of drug use in plain sight. Those things could lead cops to your door.

One weekend, Jesse-Ray talked about his father. The next weekend, he talked about Rick, his father figure. Jesse-Ray seemed to have little but contempt for his father. He expressed far more respect for Rick.

I mulled over what distinguished the two. The juxtaposition was striking. According to Jesse-Ray, the two men were starkly different. Rick, an explainer, was meticulous, but Jesse-Ray's father "did not care about anything."

As for similarities, both men were mean, exacting, and tough, and—so Jesse-Ray believed—they both loved him.

"Rick took a bullet for me once," he said, brimming with admiration and conviction. At the same time, he said, "that man could make the devil weep."

One Sunday afternoon, I arranged Jesse-Ray's descriptions of these men side by side in a poem titled "Portrait of Two Fathers." The poem sprang from Jesse-Ray's accounts of his father's sloppy running of a trap house. "It was easy for the police to catch him," Jesse-Ray told me. "Straight easy."

Not so Rick, who was crafty, savvy, glib, and sophisticated. Jesse-Ray credited Rick with teaching him the drug trade. Rick kept everything "tight and clean." Rick was careful. And, unlike Jesse-Ray's father, Rick obviously made it his business to lavish attention on Jesse-Ray—to treat him as important.

Rick even noticed Jesse-Ray's small mannerisms. "He could see when I was getting mad," Jesse-Ray said. Moments before he would burst into unreasoning anger, he would flick his tongue along his lower teeth. "Rick called it 'lickin' angry.'"

The poem about the two fathers was still printing out on our home printer when I had to drive back to Blacksburg, Virginia, for work. I didn't have time to show it to Jesse-Ray or discuss it with him, as I usually did. It was left to Hal to show Jesse-Ray the final draft. Jesse-Ray stared at it for a long time, seemingly troubled, Hal told me later. Apparently, he had never held thoughts about the two men in his mind at the same time. Both men had profoundly affected his development. But he seemed uncomfortable comparing them.

After a few moments, with Hal piling praise on him for his poetic achievement, Jesse-Ray approved the piece for inclusion in his book, which was by now almost half written. He liked seeing his poems in final form and approved them all, with "Portrait of Two Fathers" the only one he hesitated over.

It was rewarding, seeing Jesse-Ray's horizons broaden as they did in this poem. Through his poetry, he had succeeded in seeing his father and Rick in new ways.

Rick's observation was right on, too. I saw Jesse-Ray get "lickin' angry" once. His eyes went dead. His mouth parted slightly, and his tongue flicked, light and fast, along his lower teeth.

I saw it happen when Jesse-Ray was talking about being kicked out of his dad's trailer at the behest of a landlord. It was a convoluted story and, like many of Jesse-Ray's recollections, it contained gaps and things that didn't add up. Remembering the landlord's unfairness and his dad's callousness, Jesse-Ray flicked his tongue along his bottom teeth and got deathly quiet.

Abruptly, he got up and said he needed a smoke. Ten minutes later, he was back inside, sitting on the couch, relaxed again.

It turned out to be the tree punching incident.

He quickly regained his jovial mood, holding up his hand, lightly skinned at the knuckles, grinning as he boastingly proclaimed that punching a tree was "progress." In the past he would have found somebody's face to smash.

"Progress," I agreed.

But as I edited his lines of verse from afar, it was Hal doing the heavy lifting. Hal was the one who recognized that Jesse-Ray's self-esteem needed shoring up. And Hal was the one who stepped in to become his navigator when it came to social services, because Jesse-Ray had no idea where to look for help, lacking even a rudimentary understanding of what was available. Just as Jesse-Ray had acceded to his father's authority, then fallen under Rick's sway, he willingly embraced Hal's newfound role in his life.

In addition to taking Jesse-Ray to Narcotics Anonymous meetings every night and picking him up after an hour, Hal chauffeured Jesse-Ray every other place he needed to be. Hal became Jesse-Ray's eyes and ears and note-taker as they navigated various bureaucracies. They went to one office for medical benefits and another for food stamps. They stumbled across the kindly director of a nonprofit agency, Darryl Cannady of South Central

Educational Development in downtown Bluefield, who offered free condoms and sex education. Cannady even invited Jesse-Ray to stop by once or twice a week to pick up donated produce.

In pursuit of Jesse-Ray's new life, Hal and Jesse-Ray trudged to various buildings in Bluefield as well as those a half-hour away in Princeton, West Virginia, the seat of Mercer County, which resulted in Jesse-Ray signing up for college courses. His enrollment was contingent on passing placement exams. Hal took him to the college to take the exams, which were necessary for proper placement into preadmission remedial classes. When Jesse-Ray failed the exams, Hal helped him study and retake them. With Hal's help, Jesse-Ray also applied for money from the federal government to pay for tuition. Classes were scheduled to start in fall semester at the end of August, which was still several weeks away.

When Jesse-Ray continued to worry that the Bluefield Union Mission might cut short his stay in the safe house, Hal reassured him.

"Everyone is all lined up to help you. We all want you to be here, to make it," Hal said.

At the end of a particularly long day of volunteer work at the mission, topped off with a Narcotics Anonymous meeting at day's end, Hal told Jesse-Ray once again that he was proud of him.

"Can I tell you something?" Jesse-Ray asked Hal.

"Of course!"

"I think I love you, man."

Hal was touched. He had grown fond of Jesse-Ray. He willingly took on the role of mentor, role model, and father figure. One of Hal's first efforts was to stop Jesse-Ray's repeated use of the word "muh-fuckah." Jesse-Ray, eager at first to be the dwarf planet to Hal's star, did his best to curb the expression. Hal earnestly explained to Jesse-Ray that he should stop dropping the f-bomb as expletives and obscenities had no place in normal adult conversation. Jesse-Ray told me that cleaning up his language was hard but that he was trying to comply because he knew Hal was right.

One weekend, Jesse-Ray seemed particularly excited to talk to me. He had news.

"The other day, Hal called me 'son.' Blew my fuckin' mind! My first thought was, 'I'm going to fuck this up somehow.' My second thought was, 'What did I do to make him feel that way?' When someone does something for foster kids, we're so used to being left that we fuck it up. We push people away."

He continued with what sounded like a combination of fatalism and self-blame. "I don't like hurting people. I've always been bad luck. That's why I try not to get attached."

And then, curiously, with prescient self-awareness, he added, "I am so scared of hurting people. I would rather not have the chance. I'm used to blocking myself from everybody—not actually building a relationship, because I'm scared to."

"How are you dealing with the fact that Hal is in your life and willing to help?"

"I'm dealing with it."

"How?"

"I don't know," he said. "But something's different. People tried to help in the past, but I didn't want help. This time I feel weird, in the best way. It's like the feeling you get when you take your first steps. You think, 'What the fuck is going on? This is awesome! I want to keep walking. This is cool. I can move around.' And yet you're always going to fall."

I shared with him the famous forward-thinking Henry Ford quote, hoping it might bolster his attitude, "Whether you think you can, or think you can't—you're right."

During the first three bittersweet months, Hal and I held hope that the village gathering around Jesse-Ray would be enough to salvage a life headed nowhere, that love would triumph, and that Hal's unrelenting acceptance and buoying up of Jesse-Ray would bear fruit.

"Are you committed to turning your life around?" I asked.

A grin spread slowly across his face. "I'm here, ain't I?"

What teenage boys need

"The space of mentoring has been lost in our society," writes Linda Marks in Spirit of Change Magazine, pointing out that a teenage boy spends an average of thirty minutes of focused time each week with the male in his home. Compare this with the average of forty hours devoted to video games!

"Boys need good men in their lives as role models," says Craig McClain, founder of the Boys to Men Mentoring Network. "Society has missed this, saying that boys will figure things out on their own. I have asked thousands of boys what kind of man they want to be, and no one has said 'a drug dealer,' 'a bum,' 'a wife beater' or 'a gang member.' [However] boys take the choices that are available to them, if they are not given another choice."

The Boys to Men program, an international nonprofit, creates a community of role models for boys as young as eleven in which the boys are called "journeymen," and the men are called "mentors." Boys enjoy multiple role models as they gather for weekend training as well as meetings called "J-groups." Building emotional intelligence is a key goal as boys learn to show feelings, value other people, and develop trust.

Big Brothers Big Sisters is another program that attempts to fill in where families may falter. A mentor is known as "a Big" and the child is "a Little"; the organization makes the match and a one-on-one relationship is key to the concept. The group cites research on its impact: After eighteen months of mentorship, a child is 46 percent less likely to begin using illegal drugs and 52 percent less likely to skip school. Almost all those mentored reported that the relationship helped them to make better choices throughout their childhoods, and many said that the benefit extended into adulthood.

Psychologist and author Linda Phillips-Jones offers the following advice about mentoring: "Over time, help your mentees figure out how to get the most from you: what you know how to do, why you want to mentor them, the boundaries you want to set, your pet peeves, and your typical styles of communicating and thinking. Discuss how to 'read' each other and give each other feedback. Teach your mentees what mentors usually expect and help them find other mentors besides you."

Hal had never been schooled in how to be a mentor. But his instincts were surprisingly close to what the experts describe as ideal. Hal had hoped that his presence, influence, devotion of time, and caring would demonstrate to Jesse-Ray that there were many better ways to be a man than those Jesse-Ray had witnessed in his nineteen years. Hal was a devoted mentor, at least in the way that Boys to Men Mentoring Network founder McClain frames it:

"They need men who care about them, will accept them for who they are and where they are. Rather than telling them to do things differently, they need men who will listen to them and just be there for them, and accept their journey—the faults, the grace, and the glory."

In the end, Hal allowed Jesse-Ray to make his own choices, to flounder, and ultimately to flunk out of the safe house. Hal also made it clear that his friendship was unconditional and timeless; he extended an open-ended invitation for Jesse-Ray to stay in contact in the future.

CHAPTER 7

"Do you believe in God?"

I will fight to reach the light.
I have changed my life.
I feel like my heart
has finally
been treated
with tenderness.

—Jesse-Ray Lewis, "Purple"

One odd aspect of this story—curious even to me—involves the willing, almost unquestioning participation of Hal and me. How did we come to welcome Jesse-Ray and take charge of vital aspects of his life? I love my own two children (now grown), but being a stay-at-home mom was never my dream. Even as I raised my own kids during their infancy and toddlerhood, I longed for time to be alone with my writing projects and journalistic ambitions.

Hal, for his part, wanted nothing more to do with child-rearing at this stage of life. After all, we were only a few years from retirement. He and his first wife had their two children in their early twenties. Hal had planned it that way; he wanted the nest to empty early so that he could count on at least a few unfettered years to pursue his own interests.

By taking Jesse-Ray into our lives, we became a pair of unlikely pseudo-parents or godparents or whatever we were. We were less than guardians, who are appointed by courts and hold decision-making powers. We were not exactly foster parents, either, because

Jesse-Ray didn't live with us, and we didn't earn money from the state to look after him. And yet we were more emotionally invested than many foster parents who care for children in return for a paycheck and view their work as a business transaction.

Our willingness to take on Jesse-Ray and at least some of his problems probably stemmed from assumptions unique to each of us. Having made my living as a writer and editor, I could see how Jesse-Ray's writing ability could be his ticket to productivity. A strong believer in the family unit, Hal was convinced that an upstanding male role model might be all that Jesse-Ray needed to wean him from drugs and crime.

These were strong reasons and incentives for us to step in. But I believe our commitment went beyond what inspired us as individuals. Something prompted us as a pair to embark on a project that had the potential to inconvenience us, at the very least, and disrupt our lives, at the very worst.

Hal and I were different in personality, upbringing, aptitude, and choice of careers. During the 1970s, we were in Tampa and Miami, two major Florida cities, at the same time, but our paths never crossed. Sometimes I wonder about what might have happened if I'd met Hal in my early twenties. I'm not sure that I had the maturity then to appreciate his exceptional qualities. He had been through a rigorous apprenticeship at the Panama Canal shipyard and was a rigger and millwright. He was a genius with his hands, able to build tools and fix machines and diagnose problems that stymied other craftspeople. I was bent on a more academic, professional career and probably would have discounted his mechanical abilities.

When he was just three months old, his parents had moved to the Panama Canal Zone and found jobs to be close to his paternal grandparents, who had been teachers in the Canal Zone since the 1920s. Hal enjoyed their loving attention, especially since he suffered from undiagnosed learning disabilities throughout his school years. His grandparents made him feel smart even as teachers and his own mother labeled him "stupid."

I understood Hal's motives in wanting to help Jesse-Ray, and I appreciated his nurturing nature. And yet Hal's willingness to take on this immense challenge startled me. Pressed into caring for his siblings at an early age, he viewed child-rearing as unwanted drudgery. The last thing I expected was for Hal to sacrifice his hard-won freedom in favor of daily domestic responsibility. His childhood had been far from idyllic.

His mother often forced him, the oldest, to take care of the others. Sometimes she deputized him because she went to work; other times she just had other things she wanted to do. He changed diapers, gave baths, read stories, and cooked meals. He was a good, dutiful, sweet kid who didn't rebel, even though his mother would punish him if the siblings under his care got into mischief. Hal's parents were rough when it came to physical punishments. Hal remembers his mother smacking him in the face with a spatula, "just because."

I didn't spare Hal my opinion of his upbringing. I thought it was kooky. In addition to his parents thinking that beating their children was a good child-rearing practice, they also indoctrinated them in a religion that taught that they had a lock on interpreting the Bible. This included the part about the rapture: They believed that one day Christ would come to rule the earth for 1,000 years. Literally. Hal's family and church-mates were steeped in triumphalism, believing that their religion was the right one and everyone else's was wrong. When he lived in Florida, Hal's church "disfellowshipped" him because he got divorced, which seemed to me like a fancy word for ostracism—something that in my view, Jesus never practiced nor preached.

Later, one of Hal's close relatives nixed our idea that Hal and I would hold our wedding ceremony on their expansive, picturesque acreage. It was either out of disapproval over Hal's divorce or my differing religious perspective; I never found out which. We ended up getting married in a wildlife park in Tampa, a memory I cherish partly because of the ospreys that flew overhead and the rainbow that materialized. I told Hal that his church's brand of Christianity seemed overbearing and judgmental. But Hal stood fast, with strong faith in a God that had brought him much peace. He rejected his parent's wrongheaded disciplinary techniques but embraced their religious dogma.

The seminal event of Hal's childhood came when his parents sent him to Miami in 1969. He blamed his parents for pushing him out of the nest too soon. The Vietnam War was raging, and his mother was convinced that Miami would be a better place for Hal to make the case for conscious objector status, which their religion called for. The US military often denied the request, and she thought a draft board in a big city might be familiar with the concept, while such an appeal might be rejected in the Panama Canal Zone because it was so rare. Hal disagreed with her thinking but was underage and had to comply. He was sad that his parents had wrenched him away from his friends and younger brothers and sisters, whom he'd helped to raise. The Panama Canal Zone was the only home he had ever known.

On his own with no street-smarts or understanding of the wider world, he craved a helping hand, but none came. He was stranded in a major metropolitan area with no friends or relatives beyond his maternal grandparents, whom he had never felt close to, partly because they lived in Miami and partly because he found them disagreeable, even physically abusive. They even charged seventeen-year-old Hal rent.

His short stay with them came to an abrupt end one day as he was lying prone on the porch, shirtless, enjoying the Florida rays. His grandmother called for him to get out of the sun—not because she was worried he'd get sunburned but because the matron next door was ogling him. The next thing he felt was his grandmother's cane crashing down on his bare back. He gathered up his possessions and left the house to strike out on his own.

Where would he live? Would he pursue a career or continue with menial jobs? Go to school? He hardly knew where to turn. Growing up in a US enclave in Central America, he'd known only a world where no one locked their homes. Everyone trusted everyone. His small church community had provided a sense of belonging and closeness. In Miami, he felt defenseless, left to chart his own path in a big city where he soon found that not everyone could be trusted.

At the age of seventeen, forced to master the logistics of his life with no adult help, he became roommates with a co-worker, paying his share of the apartment's rent with money he'd saved.

He was tall, painfully thin, and naïve about the ways of the world, especially since throughout his Christian upbringing, his mother had deplored all things "worldly." She even objected to Hal's father's hunting and fishing trips, which Hal loved to go on, because she judged such pursuits unacceptable, even if society deemed them wholesome.

Hal viewed his Miami years as a time of shattered innocence. His view of humanity became skewed. He landed a job as a cleaner of airplanes for a major airline, and a co-worker bullied him, jealous that Hal had been accepted into the airline's mechanic apprenticeship program. This distressing experience eventually culminated in Hal punching out the bully. Hal was also exposed to the world of illicit drugs and even dabbled in drug running for a few months before heeding a friend's warning to stop.

These were not fond memories. Hal believed his years alone in Miami contaminated his nature, pulled him into unsavory activities, and gave him a hard edge, corrupting his instinct that humanity was good. In the Panama Canal Zone, people treated each other like family. If someone wanted to borrow money or anything else, you handed it over without question. Hal freely shared his material possessions, including letting friends borrow his car. In Miami he did the same, never asking where they were taking the vehicle or when they would bring it back. One day, he had to go to work, but his friends hadn't returned with his car. They hadn't even phoned. Hal's roommate was incredulous. "What are you doing lending people your car?" he asked. Hal came to realize that not everyone unquestioningly handed over their keys to any friends or acquaintances who asked.

Hal learned through trial and error that people could take advantage. Sometimes they never paid back money. Sometimes they said things that turned out to be false, or their behavior unmasked them as thugs. Once, Hal found himself in a store with a group of friendly teens, who instructed him to shoplift with them. When he said, "No! That's wrong!", the boys turned on him, threatening to kick his ass when they got outside. Forced to beat a hasty retreat, Hal was shocked that they failed to share his values about right and wrong, and he was further amazed that they had taken offense at his attempt to keep them on the straight and narrow. Suspicion took root in his consciousness, and he suffered, knowing that he must abandon his penchant for unquestioning trust. He was upset and angry at the same time because he believed in Jesus's admonitions to love thy neighbor and turn the other cheek.

But what infuriated him most was having been let loose as a teenager to fend for himself.

"I was in a big city, a seventeen-year-old who'd been told I was just a stupid kid who couldn't learn anything," he told me when we talked about his childhood. "And yet I was supposed to figure all this out for myself."

My childhood experience was the opposite of Hal's. My parents had converted to Catholicism when they married, and my siblings and I were raised Catholic. Whatever one may think of the flawed Catholic Church, it has its cerebral side, harboring many great philosophers from the mystical St. Francis of Assisi and St. Teresa of Ávila to the rigorous thinker St. Augustine. While I'm no longer a Catholic, I find much to admire in liberation theology, practiced by priests and nuns in Latin American who've harnessed civic and political life to aid the poor and oppressed. I still give money to Catholic charities, and I appreciate having been steeped in wide-ranging theological thought.

As for my nature, I was rebellious and highhanded and critical of my parents, even though my mother was kind enough to make sure that I was never saddled with undue obligations, certainly not the job of caring for my younger siblings. Second in the birth order, she herself had been older sister to two younger ones. Remembering the times she felt unfairly pressed into service and burdened with chores, she made a point of allowing me my own childhood, unencumbered.

Hal was born in Peoria, Illinois, and transported as an infant to the Panama Canal Zone. I was born in Michigan and transported to Florida, but the transfer occurred at age nine, so unlike Hal, I was aware of the move.

My father had gotten his dream job at Cape Kennedy as an electrical engineer, and only later did I realize that he was, in fact, one of the fabled rocket scientists of the space-race era. As kids growing up in a neighborhood of Satellite Beach where most of the fathers commuted north on Highway A1A to "the cape," we thought our dads were ordinary engineers. My father worked for Chrysler, and one of my best friends had a father who worked for Northrop Grumman. Another friend's father worked for Martin Marietta.

I was enthralled with the fact that the Atlantic Ocean was a ten-minute walk from our house. My friends and I would swim in the waves all summer and on weekends. Only hurricanes or the rare cold winter day put the water off limits. We also watched the frequent missile launches from our backyards, as NASA's east coast of Florida was the launch center for Apollo and Skylab missions. My father worked on the Apollo-Soyuz Test Project, the first joint US-Soviet space flight.

During our childhoods, Hal and I lived in completely different parts of the globe. In addition to geographic differences, two other big contrasts marked our coming-of-ages.

Craving autonomy and independence, I couldn't get out of the house fast enough. I got my wish for independence when I was seventeen, the same age that Hal was when his parents refused to allow him to stay in the Panama community that he viewed as a wonderful cocoon. I headed off to the University of South Florida in Tampa with a National Merit Scholarship underwriting my tuition and other college costs. Three hours away from the Space Coast where I had grown up, I felt completely on my own, and I loved the feeling. When my family moved back to Michigan after government support for the space program waned, they offered me the chance to join them and transfer to a university in Michigan. I elected to stay put. My prized independence would allow for no other choice.

By contrast, Hal resented being pushed away—he perceived the move to Miami as unmerited at best and punishing at worst. In hindsight, it seemed to me that his mother was trying to protect him. But Hal viewed his experience as a banishment. Worse, he believed that her insistence on sending him to Miami for a better shot at claiming conscientious objector status represented human scheming that flew in the face of what she'd always said about God: that God would take care of everything. One needed only to pray, to put the problem in God's hands. Whether or not the hand of God was at work, the draft board in Miami declared Hal unfit for service, but not because he was a conscientious objector. Doctors found a slight problem with his heart.

My life after college kept me in Florida, where I worked as a journalist in Tampa, while Hal began a life's journey that took him back to Panama, where he married, then to upstate New York, Oregon, Texas, and, finally, back to Florida, where we met in 2002. Hal's marriage had ended several years earlier, and I had been divorced for two. We were ready to start a new life together.

Children grown, we were free to move wherever our hearts took us. We ended up in West Virginia after I researched mountain elevations and home prices and found what looked like an affordable home in Bluefield. Florida was hot, crowded, and expensive. The mountains of Appalachia beckoned.

In 2006, two years after our marriage, we traveled north to

look at the house I'd spotted on the Internet. Though it needed major renovation, something about it captivated us at first sight. We bought it as a summer home. Hal worked on the house for the entire first summer while we stayed in a short-term rental in the nearby town of Bramwell. By summer's end, he'd completely redone the wiring and plumbing. He winterized the house, and we returned to Florida, looking forward to returning to spend the following summer.

We loved the process of working together to choose and arrange furniture and pick paint colors. We created art, coming up with zanier ideas together than we could have apart. We fed off each other's creativity. For our house in Tampa, we'd created custom drapery rods and artistic finials out of copper and clay. In Bluefield, when money was too tight for us to purchase art, we made big abstract paintings by slapping paint directly on our living room walls. Hal, ever the craftsman, measured out and meticulously painted black frames around each of our primary-colored masterpieces.

At the end of our second summer in Bluefield, which bills itself as "Nature's Air-Conditioned City" because of the cool mountain air, I found myself rooted in Appalachia. Nothing could persuade me to return to steamy Florida, but Hal headed back south to ready our Florida house for sale, doing repairs and putting it on the market. Hal was a little less enthusiastic about the move. He hadn't made his mind up about the scraggly town of Bluefield, even though I portrayed our new, permanent abode as a mountain paradise. He wasn't sure he would like living in a small town, and he was put off by the signs of economic decline—buildings in disrepair, falsely cheerful signs that touted the coal-mining industry (which had been dying for years), and virtually no employers offering well-paying jobs. But he went along with the move.

Some of my friends and family members made fun of our decision to live in West Virginia. They viewed Appalachians as politically unenlightened and culturally unsophisticated. "Why would you want to live around a bunch of toothless West Virginians?" a friend asked. I objected to their stereotypes, countering that many of the people we'd met were perfectly lovely and had all their teeth. West Virginia was a gorgeous state, with lush forests, coursing rivers, a plethora of waterfalls, and rich animal life. Octobers were breathtaking as the trees took on red and orange hues. Even though Hal and I had married on a November day in tropical Florida, which lacks orange leaves in autumn and snow in winter, we decided to move our anniversary celebration to October because we loved the brilliant fall foliage that we'd missed in years of living in always-sunny Florida. Many of West Virginia's tourism marketing messages included "four seasons" in the phrasing. When Governor Jim Justice proposed tripling West Virginia's tourism budget to $20 million in December 2017, he said, "What state could there possibly be that has four seasons like we have?"

After Hal wrapped up our remaining obligations in Tampa, we reunited in Bluefield, and he set to work insulating our house and rebuilding its walls. But our home-renovation project couldn't be his sole focus—he still needed to earn money to cover bills. He took a part-time position at Lowe's, working primarily in the plumbing and electrical departments. (Even before being employed there, he was prone to help befuddled-appearing people find what they were looking for when he was at the store; it seemed he knew the whereabouts of each of the 40,000 items Lowe's kept in stock.) In addition, he also did handyman and light-construction jobs for local clients. These outside jobs and his work on the safe house prevented the work on our own home from ever being finished.

Not long after Hal came back to Bluefield, I began to work out of town, first at West Virginia University in Morgantown (four hours away) and later at Virginia Tech in Blacksburg, a ninety-minute drive from our home. The Virginia Tech job, which started at the end of 2009, allowed me to spend almost every weekend in Bluefield. The situation suited both of us. I wasn't forced to live full-time in a home I'd fondly nicknamed "the construction zone," and Hal was spared the prospect of my being constantly underfoot and inquiring about an end date.

My work was both demanding and fulfilling, and I was grateful to live within walking distance of the campus. Hal had applied his talents in construction to my 300-square-foot apartment, and my custom-designed comforts included floor-to-ceiling shelves, a full kitchen, and a bedroom defined by attractive wooden doors and dressers. We enjoyed watching movies and cooking and hiking together on the weekends, but we were not unhappy with the weekday solitude.

I'd switched my driver license and car registration from Florida to West Virginia as soon as I could. But having lived for four decades in Florida, I didn't feel like an Appalachian, even though, like many people from the region, a strong Scots-Irish strain ran through my ancestry. After a while, I knew that I'd become more culturally attuned when I began to cringe every time an outsider to the region would refer to it as "Appa-LAY-shuh" instead of the pronunciation that native-born residents preferred, "Appa-LATCH-uh."

We cherished our Bluefield home, even though it needed major fixes such as being jacked up two inches because of the way foundations were built a century ago. Its classic bungalow-style layout worked for us, and the oak floors and staircase gave the modest home a sumptuous feel. I had always wanted to live in a two-story house and seeing mountains from almost every window was a joy.

Virtually the only downside was the house next door. Everything from loud music to the mounds of trash in the yard threatened to destroy our peace of mind. After a young couple bought the home, things settled down for a year or two. Then they moved out of state, leaving the house in the hands of a management company, which brought in tenants who were not just dirty and loud, but who also neglected their animals. At one point during an icy winter, the latest set of renters, who owned two pit bulls, had allowed their dogs' chains to become intertwined. The dogs couldn't reach their water dishes. From our upstairs windows, we could see them struggle. Hal went over to disentangle them and break the thin layer of ice atop their dishes so they could drink. When the dogs died a few weeks later after eating poison that the owners had put out in the yard to kill rats drawn by the trash they left around, we couldn't bear to think of someone equally cruel and clueless moving in.

The young absentee landlords who'd owned the house fell behind on payments, or so we heard, and the house sat empty for several months. Eventually it became a Fannie Mae, Freddie Mac property offered for sale at a rock-bottom cash price by the two US government-sponsored enterprises. We took out a loan against our home, and I took a small buy-out offer from the retirement plan of a newspaper company I'd once worked for. This money, we hoped, would finance the cost of the house along with the necessary repairs, and we concluded the purchase.

After a year of hard labor, Hal brought the lower story back up to code, and it was ready for occupancy. During that year, we had frequently stopped by the Bluefield Union Mission, which was right around the corner, to visit and catch up with Craig. From the start, Craig had been aware of our renovation project and had embraced the idea of leasing the space as a safe house. Craig loved to brainstorm, and we had considered choosing a name for the safe house from the Bible. Craig liked the sound of "Gilead House" but we dropped the idea after looking up several references and finding Gilead referred to in the Book of Hosea as "a city of those who work iniquity; it is stained with blood." That was not the tone we wanted to set!

I had never connected the thought of helping aged-out foster children with our purchase of the safe house. A year or two before the lower story was finished, I had floated the idea to Hal that it might be something we could do in retirement. I liked the idea of providing support to older teenagers after they aged out of foster care and their state support abruptly ended. With a small amount of money and a willingness to help, we could assist a former foster child finish high school or get started in community college. Hal was cool to the idea but didn't rule it out.

When the Bluefield Union Mission placed Jesse-Ray in the safe house, Hal and I were still years away from the free time that retirement might afford us; we didn't feel ready for this type of commitment, not only in terms of finances, but also because we were both still working full-time hours. And yet we forged ahead.

Maybe in the same way that we created unique artwork together, Hal and I fed off each other's interests and motives. Knowing my interest in helping aged-out foster children made Hal amenable to committing himself to Jesse-Ray's needs. For my part, I was intrigued by Hal's willingness to embrace a quasi-parental role, despite all his declarations about being free from child-rearing demands. I was eager to witness the effects of Hal's nurturing personality on a young man in need.

We'd married too late in life to have children together, and I liked seeing him in nurturing roles because his aptitude for being of service to others was one of his more admirable traits. He would spend hours fixing a motorcycle for my son, for example, or making a custom toy for my grandson. When my son-in-law was away completing the US Army's rigorous Ranger School, Hal repeatedly sent him packages of chocolate and meat, making sure there was ample booty to share with the men who had no families to provide treats.

Hal longed to be the adult role model that he had craved at Jesse-Ray's age. Despite Jesse-Ray's childhood trauma and gang-related crimes, Hal had faith that his mentorship could be effective. Jesse-Ray came across as someone whose virtue was either dormant or latent but open to flowering given the proper nourishment.

Even though I knew that Hal didn't do things halfway, his eagerness probably should have been a clue to me that complex psychological forces were motivating Hal and that—in wishing sobriety on and expecting obedience from a drug-addicted teen—

perhaps Hal was setting himself and Jesse-Ray up for failure. I ignored this and other clues because of my delight in having learned that Jesse-Ray could write and write well. If Jesse-Ray was Hal's project, he was my prodigy.

Something about Jesse-Ray's winning combination of vulnerability and street smarts, along with his uncomplicated-seeming personality, made us believe that our mentorship could be a turning point for him. He had a laid-back demeanor and disarming grin. And even though Hal had initially been cool to the idea of assisting an aged-out foster child, when Jesse-Ray materialized, Hal was wholeheartedly in favor of offering the help that we seemed able and suited to provide.

Shortly after Jesse-Ray moved into the safe house, looking for some basis to connect with him, Hal asked him, "Do you believe in God?"

Jesse-Ray, always quick on his feet, shot back, "Would I be here if I didn't?"

Eventually we realized that the answer was a classic Jesse-Ray evasion.

Jesse-Ray often countered Hal's earnestness with his own brand of cocky, youthful knowingness. He didn't hesitate to point out where he thought Hal's and my knowledge was outdated or wrong. He especially seemed to relish catching us saying something hopelessly innocent, because though we were neither saints nor naïfs, we had never moved in a tough, gang-dominated milieu as he once had. And then there were our cultural differences. He was a child of the mountains; we were "flatland ferriners."

He laughed at the lingo I used to describe illegal drugs—the language of my own college days in the hippy-dippy-trippy seventies. He also laughed at my pronunciation of Virginia towns he was familiar with—such as Richlands—which I pronounced in two fully weighted syllables. Jesse-Ray seemed to swallow the second syllable in a way I could never properly vocalize. Jesse-Ray loved being one up on us.

About a month into Jesse-Ray's stay, Hal found a way to have the last word. First, he told Jesse-Ray about our initial plan to help aged-out foster children. Then he informed him that we'd projected to be doing that a few more years in the future. Hal further impressed upon Jesse-Ray that the typical protocol of the Bluefield Union Mission was to provide lodging to someone for only two or three nights. Yet Craig had made an executive decision, an on-the-spot dispensation, allowing Jesse-Ray to stay in the safe house indefinitely.

"The minute I finished renovating that safe house, you came walking out of the woods looking for a new life and a place to stay," Hal concluded, smiling smugly. "Are you telling me you don't see the hand of God at work?"

Jesse-Ray didn't answer.

Appa-LAY-shuh versus Appa-LATCH-uh: Outsiders revealed

Move to the mountains and you soon learn that a region with a chip on its shoulder wants to be called by its right name.

The word "Appalachia" is open to several pronunciations. Stick a strong "a" sound in the middle, and you are immediately pegged an outsider. Appa-LAY-shuh or Appa-LATCH-uh may be the two most common, but here are six publicized by West Virginia Public Radio:

1. Appa-LAT-cha

2. Appalach-EE-a

3. Appalay-CHEE-uh

4. Appalay-SHUH

5. Appala-shuh

6. Appalay-SHE-ya

Anita Puckett, director of Appalachian Studies at Virginia Tech, recounts an incident that shows the issue can rankle. She once took students on a folk-culture field trip during which they visited a potter, originally from Illinois, who'd been working in the region for more than two decades.

The artisan was knowledgeable and shared lore about Southern Appalachian pottery making. One of Puckett's students, a native of southwest Virginia, dismissed the man's contribution in a conversation after the visit, discounting everything the potter had said. The potter's crime? He employed the Appa-LAY-shuh pronunciation. Unsurprised by the student's emotional reaction, Puckett pointed out that Noah Webster, in the 1828 edition that became America's first authorized dictionary, omitted the word "Appalachia." Instead, Webster defined the region by the term Northerners favored, "the Alleghenies"—an editorial act of aggression that Puckett labelled political.

Alan "Cathead" Johnston, a folk singer and coal miner's son from rural McDowell County, West Virginia, points out the absurdity of many self-appointed outsiders who seek to shine a spotlight on Appalachia. He sings about how outsiders can't even pronounce the name of the region properly, yet they are "gonna tell the world all about me!"

According to scholars at the University of South Carolina:

"Some people would say that, if you come to the region and say 'Appa-LAY-cha,' you might as well turn around and make tracks to wherever you started from. In a short essay published thirty years ago in Appalachian Heritage, one Eastern Kentuckian wrote, 'What I finally came to understand is that Appa-LAY-cha does not exist . . . It is an idea created by politicians and reporters.' You wouldn't want to tangle with him."

You also might not want to tangle with bestselling author Sharyn McCrumb, who writes, "Appa-LAY-shuh is the pronunciation of condescension, the pronunciation of the imperialists, the people who do not want to be associated with the place, and the pro-nunciation Appa-LATCH-uh means that you are on the side that we trust."

Some writers refer to the Appalachian mountain dialect as Scottish-flavored Elizabethan English. In addition to Scotland and England, a third dialectical influence came from 16th century Spanish explorers, who infiltrated Florida and appropriated a Native American name for an Indian village there, Apalache. Spanish and French mapmakers, ignorant of the topography of eastern Northern America, slapped the "Apalache" moniker on the entire Southern mountain region.

Tessa McCoy-Hall, originally from southwest Virginia, writes:

"The pronunciation of Appalachia is much more than 'You aren't from around here, are you?' or memes on our newsfeeds telling us which is the correct pronunciation and which is not. From Georgia to Maine, from 'Ap-uh-latch-uh' to 'Ap-uh-lay-chuh' and every variation in between, each is our unique way of speaking which says, 'This is my history. This is where I am from. This is where my ancestors are from.' Now, I take my muddy boots off at the door of every mountain home I meet, because the pronunciation of Appalachia is a dialectal feature, not a war cry."

CHAPTER 8

Flashbacks from the drug world

I go
from watching bodies decay
to trying to pray
not to a god
but a form of my worst fears,
my every tear.

I'm stuck in thoughts.
They slowly crawl out
of my Play-Doh-like
brain.
A burnt carcass.
Maybe I'm not insane.

—Jesse-Ray Lewis, "Forgive Me"

Sometimes, we wondered about the veracity of Jesse-Ray's words. Would we ever be able to separate truth from exaggeration? Just as Jesse-Ray's co-workers at the Bluefield Union Mission thought he was lying when he said his dad would hit him with a baseball bat to make him sleep at night, Hal and I also heard things that seemed outlandish: tales of torture and violence, beatings and killings, gang oaths and gang riches. Some assertions seemed incredible, such as the hundreds of thousands of dollars that Jesse-Ray supposedly spent as part of his share of drug-trade largesse. I grilled him on these topics, trying to extract the truth.

Once, Jesse-Ray complained to Hal that I asked too many questions.

"How do you stand it?" he asked Hal, implying that life with me must be difficult because I was so inquisitive. Hal explained that I was a journalist by training and that my questions were important because they were central to the creation of the chapbook of poems that Jesse-Ray was writing.

Decades of experience doing newspaper interviews had put me in close proximity to many people whose statements turned out to be lies. But unlike those people, Jesse-Ray's demeanor didn't seem like that of a scammer or someone delusional. One weekend afternoon after Jesse-Ray had been in the safe house for about five or six weeks, he and I stood in the front yard. He was finishing a cigarette before going inside for our scheduled interview. On the agenda was a discussion of his former life as a gang member, so the moment seemed the right time to make a quick observation.

To increase the chances of hearing unvarnished truth about the gangs, I said, "You know, we'd be helping you even if you didn't have a past as a meth cook with a big-time drug-dealing gang. You could be just a kid from a small town who needed help, and Hal and I and the Bluefield Union Mission would still be providing food and shelter and helping you get into college and all the rest."

He nodded, looking thoughtful, but said nothing in response.

Some of his stories had the ring of truth. But as we settled in for our talk that afternoon, the events he described were more bizarre than anything I'd heard before.

Many of the memories that troubled him involved the illegal drug trade. After leaving the Virginia foster-care system, Jesse-Ray had gone to work for a big-time meth dealer—the man he called Rick, who ran a gang that operated in several states. Gang members were often on the move, sometimes cooking meth, other times arranging for big-money deals to drop and occasionally inflicting punishment on those who stole drugs or refused to pay. Jesse-Ray became a trusted lieutenant. In some of the stories he reported to Rick. In other versions, he worked his way up the ladder, and Rick and he were equals.

He explained that to be accepted into the gang, half a dozen other men beat him up, severely. His assailants wore metal accessories to protect themselves and to make the beating worse. Afterwards, Jesse-Ray couldn't walk and was in pain for weeks.

"Every step I took hurt," he said.

"Why would they do that?" I asked.

Jesse-Ray looked at me like I was crazy. The answer was so obvious to him that I must have appeared dense. And yet, to his credit, he patiently explained the hazing ritual to me, a person who had no concept of the weird bylaws that propped up this malignant underworld.

Being "beaten into the gang" was done so that members—homies, he called them—would become inseparable, closer than family, more bonded than lovers, and emotionally and psycho-logically intertwined in ways that eliminated any chance of betrayal. Submitting to a savage beating of his own free will demonstrated that he would never give up his compadres to the police or anyone else.

After the beating, he was one of them. He would die for them, and they for him. Or such was the moral of the story, as told by Jesse-Ray.

"They got me drunk as shit and high as shit after," he added.

In addition, Rick also schooled Jesse-Ray in the philosophy and practicalities of the drug trade. Blood, for instance.

"Blood is everything," Jesse-Ray said, becoming animated, as he often did when repeating Rick's philosophies and life lessons. "Blood is everything," he repeated. "It means family. Without blood in your body, you can't live. But one speck of blood could change your whole world." The latter reference was to Rick's fastidiousness when it came to crime-scene evidence. A crew always came in behind Rick's crime scenes, meticulously scrubbing the incriminating molecules away.

"If he was so careful to erase the evidence, then how is it that you can talk about this to me?"

Jesse-Ray's answer sent chills up my spine.

Jesse-Ray said that he hadn't made the decision to talk about his life on his own. He had consulted Rick.

"Rick knows all about you." The way Jesse-Ray said it, it sounded like a boast.

In that instant I felt nauseated. I knew that the stakes were suddenly much higher, that the law of unintended consequences might kick in, in a lethal way—and at the same time, I understood completely that nothing could be done about it.

Rick knew about me and Hal and the safe house.

Jesse-Ray told me that he had been reading his poems to Rick over the landline at the nearby convenience store. The safe house didn't have a phone, and even if it did, gang protocol demanded that Jesse-Ray call from an untraceable locale. How had I not foreseen this? Of course Jesse-Ray had sought permission to tell his story; he would have been breaking the code of silence had he shared his experiences without Rick's approval. Rick had granted permission for our writing projects to continue as long as Jesse-Ray employed false names and locations to keep Rick and his operations incognito.

Jesse-Ray—who said he would die before he'd betray his homies—had casually betrayed me and Hal. Me, the ex-journalist and now author and editor, asking questions, seeking documentation, probing, following lines of inquiry, ferreting out facts . . . I hesitated to think where this might lead. I had grilled Jesse-Ray about his past to help him put together his poems. And, by this time, I also planned to write a book of my own about Jesse-Ray's sojourn through Bluefield and his intersection with our lives. Jesse-Ray knew details that, even with names and locations fudged, constituted evidence of crimes that might prove powerful in court if a prosecutor decided to go after Rick, the architect of an interstate meth-dealing operation. The facts now baked into Jesse-Ray's poetry were incriminating. Jesse-Ray had already said enough to suggest he could be a powerful witness in court against Rick and others. The sorts of crimes they committed were unspeakable ones—the ones where statutes of limitations did not apply. I was not comfortable with Rick knowing about the books. But Jesse-Ray had taken that decision out of my hands.

Jesse-Ray assured me that Rick did not know the exact location of the safe house. This fact was no relief because, after all, how hard would it be to track down Hal, Jesse-Ray's mentor, or me, Jesse-Ray's editor? Bluefield is a small Appalachian town where the railroad cars still carry coal and where town leaders barely trotted out enough residents to make 10,000 in the last census. No one could stay hidden here for long, certainly not with clues scattered around like cigarette butts by a big-mouthed nineteen-year-old.

I would have felt better if I could have talked to Rick myself. In writing a narrative, I knew how to camouflage, disclosing just enough facts to convey the truth of a situation while still protecting the central figure. Years of journalistic training and experience had given me that. I'd interviewed plenty of people either accused or convicted of crimes, and I'd kept the identities of many sources under wraps. But with Jesse-Ray as an intermediary, I couldn't be sure that Rick understood my storytelling competence; momentarily, I felt threatened. At the same time, the damage was done. There was no going back and no sense worrying. With many more questions to ask about Jesse-Ray's gang life, I resolved to move on.

But before letting the subject change, he insisted on trying to allay my concerns.

"Rick has my back," he said, his voice taking on the familiar boastful timbre. Jesse-Ray was convinced that Rick loved him and that Rick's loving protection would therefore extend to Hal and me.

We were safe from gangs and gangsters and gang violence. We were safe from repercussions. I didn't believe Jesse-Ray's assurances. If Rick was a ruthless mastermind, as Jesse-Ray had portrayed him, then Rick wouldn't hesitate to go after potential witnesses.

"If Rick's what you say he is, if he thought you had information that could send him to prison, he'd have you killed," I said.

"If Rick was going to kill me, he'd do it himself. He wouldn't send someone to do it," Jesse-Ray asserted.

"Well, that's a fine consolation!" I cried.

I suggested that Jesse-Ray take a smoke break, which he was always willing to do. As he headed for the front door, I took a deep breath and tried to put Rick out of my mind.

Later that day, when I told Hal what Jesse-Ray had disclosed, it turned out Hal already knew. He'd been furious, and he'd told Jesse-Ray that he couldn't believe he'd exposed us to potential danger. But, like me, he knew the damage was done. However fearsome a figure Rick might be, worrying wouldn't help. Hal had kept the news from me to spare me the anxiety. As things turned out, the weeks passed without incident, and it appeared that Rick did not have us on his radar.

When Jesse-Ray came back from his smoke break, he sat down on our living-room couch in blue jeans that brushed the floor, wearing his ever-present beanie over his thick curls. He was seemingly untroubled by having disclosed our identities to Rick. What tormented him were the memories welling up from the past year.

He recounted things he'd witnessed and things he'd done. He described some activities coolly and matter-of-factly. But when he'd been forced to hurt someone or watch others inflict suffering, those nightmare scenarios haunted him, becoming recurring memories that preyed on his mind.

He'd been a meth cook, drug dealer, and all-around enforcer. The work had its perks; he'd enjoyed the money, of course. He claimed to have possessed a credit card without limits. He talked of piling hundreds of dollars' worth of merchandise into a shopping cart without worrying about the prices. At one point, living somewhere outside Virginia, he owned a car. He even owned a house. But the material goods came at a cost.

His expression changed, his face contorted, and his eyes grew distant. It was clear he was more than a witness to the drug-world dramas. He'd been a participant. He'd hurt people or at least stood by while they were being tortured. This much I believe, even though parts of his stories might have been fabrications. Guilt seemed to attach to him like the wild grape vines choking the black walnut trees on our hillside.

Fundamentally, Jesse-Ray was a tender soul. He didn't seem to have any personal goals; he didn't talk about wanting an education or a career. The only motivating factor he expressed repeatedly was the desire to repudiate his old self, to quit being a person capable of doing damage to another human.

Were there murders? Shootings? Stabbings? Threats? People left for dead? Children caught in crossfire? I don't know. I can only attest to the pain Jesse-Ray reflected in talking about his past and the agony that boiled up in the imagery of his poems.

One poem contained the ghastly image of a person with "eyes gouged out and replaced with needles," the victim's mouth slashed and "a pipe placed inside."

I gave his poems titles such as "Mental War" and "Torment" and "Pain" and "Demons" to capture the tone of his creations. His poems were as unpolished as they were powerful. In "Torment" he penned lines about a man's burned-out retinas, but Jesse-Ray-the-poet had no compassion, no desire for anything except to force the victim to "see the darkness I see."

In "The Casket," he described a maggot-infested cesspit that smelled like burning flesh. Could Jesse-Ray have invented his own Dante-esque scenarios? Perhaps. But writers rarely make things up out of whole cloth. When the writing resonates, kernels of truth can usually be found.

In the poem "Pain," he painted an image of himself that I found completely believable; he saw himself as a "flower roasting in the sun, wilting." The image made me sad for him, but I believed it accurately reflected his despairing state of mind.

He sent the lines and the rhymes to me for editing, and when I opened the files in the morning, I never knew what I was going to read. Often it was painful. The ride was always wild.

Could Jesse-Ray have invented such haunting images without a frame of reference? Did real life anchor his writing life? How much was first-hand experience, how much fantasy? From where did those images emerge—the vomit and blood and barbed wire and terrors that found their way into Jesse-Ray's poems?

The poem "Blue" gave a clue. Jesse-Ray's aversion to blue was irrational. The color caused him discomfort. He didn't want it in his line of sight.

I asked him why.

"I've lost people," he said. He'd seen friends killed by rival gangs whose gang color was blue. (Jesse-Ray's gang colors were red and black.) But through further conversation, it became clear the association went further back in time. Even in childhood the color disturbed him.

"I don't like fuckin' blue," he said, as if his vehemence explained everything. "It makes me angry. It makes me sad. My grandma would tell me if I saw anything blue I would get mad and tear it up."

Was it trauma from his early childhood or the gang violence of his later adolescence that scarred him so badly that a simple hue provoked a visceral reaction? Did real-life events evoke feelings of shame or torment? Or did Jesse-Ray's misery emerge from a single source: his own tumultuous and troubled mind?

Street-level gangs connect with violent drug lords

Jesse-Ray Lewis hinted at underworld violence when he talked about his time in the drug trade. His poems alluded to torture, beatings, even murder. He spoke of trap houses and deal drops, of wads of money that paid for spacious houses and fancy cars.

Once, on a spring afternoon, he remarked on a smell in the air, which triggered a memory. It reminded him of the odor outside a house where he once cooked meth.

A particularly excruciating memory for him involved the tragic fate of a child caught in gunfire, to which he was an eyewitness—an incident he spoke of but never dealt with in his writing.

Were his descriptions true? To some people, they seem far removed from possibility. And yet they eerily mirror reality on the ground in the United States today.

Sylvia Longmire, a consultant on Mexico's drug war, is a former special agent with the Air Force Office of Special Investigations. She also worked as a senior intelligence analyst and border security expert for California's state government. She sees drug-related violence in Mexico, which has killed tens of thousands of people, ultimately spilling into the United States.

"Granted, most of the people being tortured, kidnapped or killed have historically been criminals involved in the drug trade. However, that's changing. We're seeing more and more innocent bystanders, including children, being gunned down as collateral damage," she states.

So why aren't US news outlets reporting on such things each day? Longmire explains that Mexican cartels keep a low profile so they can blend into US society.

"Drawing attention to cartel operations in the United States is very bad for business . . . A big shootout in a San Diego shopping district or downtown Houston between heavily armed cartel gun-men and the US Army isn't going to happen anytime soon."

And the horrific violence depicted on TV and in movies? Is it true? Longmire recounts bloody incidents within US borders, including a 2009 case where five mutilated bodies were found outside a drug stash house in a well-to-do county in northern Alabama. In addition, dozens of law enforcement officers have been shot at, some severely injured, as heavily armed men protected marijuana crops in Oregon, Tennessee, North Carolina, and other states.

"Gang members from 'Los Palillos' were indicted in the kidnapping, torture and murder of nine people in San Diego County," Longmire adds, describing another incident in 2009. "Two of those victims were dissolved in vats of acid after they were killed."

During 2016, the US State Department issued travel warnings to twenty-three Mexican states—encompassing roughly three-quarters of Mexico. This included the popular tourist destinations of Cancún in Quintana Roo and Cabo San Lucas in Baja California Sur. In many parts of Mexico, US government employees are not allowed to travel from city to city after dark because of the threat of violent crime.

Could Jesse-Ray Lewis really have hooked up with a big-time drug trafficker? Such connections do exist. Members of Mexican cartels are operating in hundreds of US cities and thousands of smaller communities, according to the US Department of Justice's National Drug Intelligence Center.

The extent of opioid use in Appalachia is astounding. Headlines about the opioid epidemic dominate news websites worldwide. The 2017 Oscar-nominated Netflix documentary "Heroin(e)" focuses on drug overdoses in Huntington, West Virginia, prompting a deluge of media requests to Huntington City Hall from news teams as far away as Switzerland and Japan, seeking to chronicle affairs in the so-called overdose capital of the United States.

Michael P. Botticelli, director of the Office of National Drug

Control Policy, reported to Congress in 2015 that criminal org-anizations in Mexico "remain the greatest criminal drug threat to the United States" because these organizations "traffic heroin, methamphetamine, cocaine, and marijuana throughout the United States."

Even small neighborhood gangs continue to form relationships with these big Mexican organizations—including the most violent cartels. The Mexican drug lords supply drugs, create distribution channels and transportation networks, help enforce drug payments, and protect one gang from another. This system works for the Mexican cartels as well as for the gangs, because America's "street-level gangs . . . have a pre-existing customer base for drug distribution."

Jesse-Ray rubbed shoulders with the man who was his boss—the man he called Rick. But he never saw or spoke to anyone higher up in the trade. Does this call his entire account into question?

Not necessarily.

"In this part of the meth market, production is typically a few steps removed from the actual cartel," explains Dylan Matthews in a Washington Post piece comparing the TV series "Breaking Bad" with real life. It is common practice for the cartels to subcontract the work, insulating the cartels from anyone who might finger them. So even though the fictional "Breaking Bad" meth-cook Jesse Pinkman once met a cartel leader, it's highly unlikely that Jesse-Ray Lewis would have ever seen one in the flesh—even if his high-rolling meth-cooking tales were true.

CHAPTER 9

Jesse-Ray's recurring dream

His pleas mean nothing to me.
I feed on them.
I love to hear the scream
dream of the pain I've experienced
try to get rid of it through him
as he chokes on puke and blood

—Jesse-Ray Lewis, "Torment"

It was a Saturday. We were in my car, driving to a day-long writers' conference at a community college. I hoped the conference would elevate Jesse-Ray's ambitions. He would hear talks and rub shoulders with writers, learning that they were not a mythical class of highfalutin artists but were people like him. We had a forty-five-minute drive ahead of us. Jesse-Ray sat in the passenger seat, drank his energy drink, and launched into a description of two of his dreams.

The first, which he'd had recently, was short.

In this dream, he put a quarter into a bubble-gum machine and, to his delighted astonishment, two ladies-of-the-night emerged—a redhead and a blonde. This dream carried a comic-book quality.

"I wonder," I said to him. "Could it be that you're ready for adult appetites but not responsibilities? Clearly, you've left childhood behind. And yet you still see women as objects that exist for your pleasure. You're not relating to women as equals. You're not seeking a mature relationship with a woman but rather an exploitive one."

Jesse-Ray gave me a quizzical look. Hal was usually the sounding board for such subjects. Jesse-Ray had even told Hal about his visits to a woman who lived near the Bluefield Union Mission. He had started seeing this woman after his girlfriend from high school broke up with him because she was tired of him nagging about her drug use and bored with his constant worrying. She wanted to be stoned and carefree—at least that was Jesse-Ray's understanding. At first, he took the breakup hard. Then he referred to his ex-girlfriend in vulgar terms, saying he was glad to be rid of her.

We didn't know whether this new paramour was one of the younger sex workers who lived within walking distance of the safe house or a woman with whom he'd developed deeper ties. Probably the former, because he referred to her as "a Spanish girl who lives over there on Highland." According to Jesse-Ray, she had a child and her own house. He never called her his girlfriend.

Far more sinister was the mood of his second dream—a complex, recurring thing which haunted him. The dream's sequence was identical each time.

Jesse-Ray is in the woods with Rick in a familiar place where they would hang out when they weren't cooking meth or dealing drugs. Another comrade is there, a guy who doesn't talk much. The three are standing next to Jesse-Ray's car, a Mercedes.

They begin to walk on the trail away from the car, out of the woods. Jesse-Ray is ahead of the other two, glancing back now and then as he talks to Rick. As he nears the edge of the woods, he glances back and is astounded to see that Rick and the other guy have vanished.

This makes him sweat. Where could they have gone? He hikes back down the trail to his Mercedes. He decides to drive back to the trap house, thinking they can meet up again. He slides behind the wheel and drives along, smoking a cigarette.

Suddenly he realizes he isn't driving a car. Rather, he is sitting in a brand-new recliner in his father's trailer. (His father had never owned a recliner, much less a new one, according to Jesse-Ray. In fact, they never had much furniture.) Jesse-Ray is still smoking, but instead of flicking ash from a car window, the ashes are scattering onto the floor.

Realizing where he is, he thinks, "I've got to get out of here."

He stands up, and something he didn't realize was in his lap falls to the floor: Two weighty packages—a pound of meth and a pound of weed. Again, the feeling of urgency hits, and he knows he must act.

He takes the contraband into his boyhood bedroom and hides it, but not before packing up an ounce of meth and an ounce of weed for his own use later. He leaves the trailer, walks out on the wooden deck and then heads down the steps. When his feet hit the ground, suddenly he is back on the trail—but Rick and the other guy are still gone.

I was beguiled by the dream's circular action and rich symbolism. I offered Jesse-Ray some interpretations, explaining that they were merely suggestions and my insights might not ring true to him.

"Your mind is speaking to you in images," I offered. "This is a message from deep within your consciousness. It's clear. The life Rick offered you was something you should walk away from, pronto!"

Jesse-Ray looked skeptical, so I brought up the timing. "Look. On some level, you had that figured out inside a week. You said you first had the dream just days into your work with Rick. Some part of your mind knew that the criminal life was bad news. The violence you were forced into was torture for you. But look what happens in the dream. When you try to leave that life, you end up back in your old life, in your dad's trailer. You don't successfully escape."

Jesse-Ray gave me a sidelong glance but stayed silent as I developed the hypothesis.

"Your dad's trailer was a place of poverty, neglect, violence, and abuse. You never felt safe there. In real life, you desperately wanted to get away from it. And yet in the dream, there you are, catapulted right back."

Jesse-Ray didn't argue, so I pointed out the other symbols, attaching potential meanings to the recliner, the illegal drugs, and his childhood room.

Bringing a new recliner to the trailer showed that Jesse-Ray brought something new and valuable to his former situation—he was no longer a child, and his material possessions showed an earning power that had outstripped his dad's. Even though he had the trailer to himself in the dream, was Jesse-Ray truly free? His next action was to stand up. A weight dropped from Jesse-Ray's shoulders as the illegal drugs hit the floor. But he was not ready to relinquish the old life completely, as he had decided to hide the drugs and carve out a small stash for himself. Then he tried to take charge of his life, set a new direction, and walk out of the trailer, leaving childhood behind for good. But when his feet touched the ground, he was back on the trail—Rick's trail. But this time he was alone and without purpose or allies.

"It's an endless loop," I told Jesse-Ray. "I'm not a professional, but it looks that way to me. A dream is information that your mind, your intuition, is sharing with you through pictures and symbols. You don't fully believe that you can take charge of your life and change your future. At the moment of the most extreme uncertainty, when you return to the trail and don't know what's coming next, that's when you wake up."

Jesse-Ray said nothing. He couldn't dispute the truth that he had, indeed, made a choice to leave Rick's employ. And yet the jury was still out on whether his new life would mark a break from the bonds of childhood poverty, abuse, and the criminality that had surrounded him.

He stared straight ahead even as we took a left into the curve of the long, uphill driveway to the gleaming new college building where the conference was taking place. We didn't speak of his dreams again that day.

The next morning, we invited Jesse-Ray over for Sunday breakfast. After we'd eaten, I asked him if he'd thought about his dreams and my analysis.

"Yeah. I thought about it last night."

"How did it make you feel?"

"It was scary."

"What scares you?"

He shifted around in the dining room chair. "That it could have meaning," he said, brushing hair out of his eyes. He shrugged. "I thought it was just a dream."

Our conversation, it turned out, had been a revelation.

Child Protective Services–do they keep children safe?

More than 3 million referrals of suspected child abuse or neglect came in to state child-welfare systems in 2014, up 14.6 percent since 2010. As a result, almost 242,000 children were placed in foster care. Foster care isn't always related to abuse, however; children can end up in foster homes if a parent dies, is jailed, or suffers from addiction.

Who blows the whistle on child abusers? In most cases, it's a professional: someone from law enforcement or a doctor, nurse, or teacher. Relatives also call state hotlines and, in a small number of cases, so do friends and neighbors. Rarely does the alleged victim report the abuse, even if they are old enough to articulate what has happened.

Victims of child abuse and sexual abuse are more likely to become involved in crime as well as teen pregnancy, suicide, smoking, early-age drinking, interpersonal violence, and risky sexual behavior.

Antonio Garcia is an assistant professor of social policy at the University of Pennsylvania and a former child protective services worker in Washington State. He argues that child protective services workers labor under staggering caseloads and thus engage in tactics that may be ill informed and lack demonstrated success, documented by research.

He calls for practical improvements, such as better training for caseworkers and supervisors. Such workers must understand three things:

- The characteristics of the populations they serve;

- Effective anti-abuse practices; and

- How to deliver the right services (or how to help clients find others services that can help).

Front-line workers also need training to spot cases that need more urgent intervention.

Investment in preventive efforts would save not only children's lives but also money, Garcia says. Child abuse costs the nation approximately $124 billion annually, measured in health-care dollars, productivity losses, and public underwriting of child welfare services and criminal justice procedures.

Deploying resources to the areas of greatest need must include hiring more staff to manage high caseloads. Innovative programs and services must be underwritten as well; states can take advantage of federal funds to expand evidence-based child-welfare interventions that may have previously been underfunded.

CHAPTER 10

The richest homeless man in Bluefield

They had lives that
didn't involve
walking miles
every day
and living in abandoned houses
dealing drugs
and being high.

I thought, I want that.
I want to live without walking
from nowhere to nowhere.

—Jesse-Ray Lewis, "Walking"

Despite Jesse-Ray's willingness to tell his life story, the narrative still had a few gaps. Seminal incidents stood out, but Jesse-Ray's memory of times and dates was sketchy. He rarely put things in context. To nail down the order of events of his life, I asked him to walk me through the sequence again and again.

"I've told you this before!" he would declare in frustration, but I pleaded for patience. True, he'd described the landmark events leading to his independence, but never within a coherent timeline. I spent a lot of time trying to piece his story together in chronological order. I knew that we had to talk about his departure from foster care, his employment with Rick, the last time he saw his father, and what had happened when he appealed to his aunt for help. He also needed to explain how he got to Bluefield. Did he walk, drive, hitchhike? And why had he hung around homeless all winter before seeking help from the Bluefield Union Mission?

We started with his final foster-care arrangement, which had disintegrated partly—but not entirely—over the marijuana charge. Jesse-Ray claimed that while in the custody of the foster parents, he often slept elsewhere, hanging out with his "homies," showing up at the house only when a social worker dropped by to check on things. He said he'd made a deal with the foster parents, who agreed to his terms.

"Why would they let you dictate terms? Because you were big and bullheaded?"

He gave a lopsided grin. "They saw that it would work out better for everyone if they let me do what I wanted," he said. Jesse-Ray had a way of implying more menace in his statements than the words conveyed.

Jesse-Ray had sized them up, guessing correctly that their life was complicated enough without engaging in a power struggle with an obstinate teen foster child, a young man intent on getting his own way.

Then came the marijuana incident. After finding pot on Jesse-Ray's bed, the foster parents called the police. We knew from court records that this happened in August 2016.

He reiterated that he didn't blame them for turning him in. He also didn't blame them for turning him out of their home. He reserved that anger for the social worker, who apparently was trying to enforce Virginia law in ousting Jesse-Ray from his foster-care placement.

More than six months before the marijuana arrest, when Jesse-Ray had turned eighteen in January 2016, the social worker had pressured him to find a job. He needed either to be gainfully employed, living in his own apartment, or both. By the summer, he had achieved neither.

Jesse-Ray looks grim in the moments after he learned the Bluefield Union Mission had cut short his stay in the safe house; behind him is the abandoned house where he squatted before seeking help at the mission.

Jesse-Ray smokes a cigarette on the steps of the abandoned house where he sought temporary shelter when he first arrived in Bluefield.

Jesse-Ray, photographed by Hal Gibson, who managed
to coax a smile from him.

Author Andrea Brunais.

Discarded furniture littered the grounds of the abandoned home
where Jesse-Ray camped out.

Left, Craig Hammond, executive director of the Bluefield Union Mission,
who sponsored Jesse-Ray's stay in the safe house. Right, Hal Gibson, Jesse-
Ray's mentor. Background, mission staff member Lamont Veal looks on.

Jesse-Ray lights a cigarette on the plastic bucket he referred to as
his living room chair near the abandoned house.

She said she would take him to a homeless shelter and, in Jesse-Ray's recounting, set a departure date. His tenure with the foster family was over.

Rather than be carted off by a social worker, he took off on foot, finding refuge in the home of a female friend. But her boyfriend disliked him, and the arrangement fell apart within a month.

That's when Jesse-Ray called Rick.

"Why on earth?" I asked. "You knew what that meant. You knew what kind of life Rick would drag you into." Jesse-Ray's foster brother already had dealings with Rick and had introduced them. Jesse-Ray knew exactly what Rick did for a living.

"I called him because he'd give me money and whatever else."

Jesse-Ray hooked up with Rick in a total-immersion kind of way, working for him, traveling out of state, owning a fancy house, acting the part of a well-heeled drug dealer. Then reality set in.

"A whole bunch of shit happened," he said, loath to relive the brutal particulars. I knew this involved Jesse-Ray becoming a party to violence—being armed, exacting payments, and carrying out rough justice. Then one day, he decided to give up the life. He'd seen one too many bloody crime scenes, and he couldn't bear the crime and terror any longer.

"I couldn't keep doing what I was doing. I was tired of being high and not giving a shit. I left, went back to Virginia."

He said he took a flight back home. He wouldn't say who paid for it, but according to him, money was no problem in those days. He was flush until his credit card was suddenly cut off.

No longer in Rick's employ, he went to his aunt's house, who feigned welcome at first but wouldn't let him stay. Despite my pressing for details, Jesse-Ray did not convey this anecdote in a way that fully made sense. Once again, he was characteristically vague when it came to his relationships and how they broke apart. He couldn't explain her rejection, but he referred to a history of bad blood between him and her husband. Apparently, Jesse-Ray had knocked him out once. Jesse-Ray said it happened in the name of protecting his aunt from domestic violence.

While conversing with his aunt, he had pointedly declined to ask about his dad, who lived nearby. Nevertheless, she called him. Eventually, Jesse-Ray ended up back in the trailer where his dad lived, alongside Jesse-Ray's uncle and his dad's girlfriend.

"His bitchy-ass girlfriend," Jesse-Ray called her. "An alcoholic who sits around drinking all day."

"Why did you go? You had a terrible history with your dad."

"Because he's my dad and I didn't have anything else," he replied.

Jesse-Ray relayed these events as though they had occurred outside his control, with the older adults making decisions for him. This made me think that Jesse-Ray couldn't grasp the concept of his own agency. Instead of taking charge of his life, he saw himself as a passive recipient of whatever happened. Instead of planting seeds, he watched, seemingly helpless, as weeds sprang up to choke him.

According to Jesse-Ray, his dad rented a trailer as part of a "company town" working arrangement. The company towns of old provided all the housing stock, allowing workers to live there, but did not permit them to own their homes. Jesse-Ray was allowed to stay with his father as long as he worked in the landlord's coal mine. Company towns sprang up throughout the minefields of Appalachia in the 20th century, establishing a landscape of servitude and oppression, with widows and orphans turned out of the homes after husbands and fathers were killed in mine accidents.

Jesse-Ray believed that the arrangement smacked of modern-day enslavement, but he agreed to perform the requested manual labor at first. He quickly tired of the situation when all he got in return was room and board—no paycheck. "I was there for months, and I didn't see a single penny. My payment was living with my hellhole dad in a shitty trailer in the middle of nowhere."

Soon, he soured on the arrangement. But again, Jesse-Ray couldn't articulate a plausible reason why things fell apart. It wasn't as if Jesse-Ray had anywhere else to go, and he didn't leave because he wanted to. He left because he was kicked out. Shortly after he refused to work for the landlord's business, the cycle of eviction came to pass. Again, Jesse-Ray was forced to seek accommodation elsewhere. He turned to his father for help.

"I asked him, 'Hey, you know anybody I could crash on their couch?' My dad said, 'No, fuck you. Call somebody who cares.' So I went to the fucking police station."

I blinked, eyes wide. I knew what a monumental statement that was, coming from Jesse-Ray. He was neutral about a lot of things, but not police, for whom he exhibited contempt at best and loathing at worst. Dracula would sooner go to a tanning salon than Jesse-Ray to a precinct.

It turned out, of course, that he didn't go to the police station. His friend went for him.

Jesse-Ray had one friend he could call—the friend who picked him up from his dad's trailer. It was this friend who eventually talked to the police.

But first, Jesse-Ray tried his aunt's house again. She shut the door in his face.

"Why?" I knew the question would get on his nerves, like it always did.

"Hell if I know." He refused to elaborate.

"Why didn't your friend take you to his home?"

"He was married. Plus he had small children. Their house was too small. I don't know."

But the friend had an idea. He drove to the police station in Richlands, Virginia, parking across the street from the cop shop.

"You don't have to go in there," he told Jesse-Ray. "I'll go ask where homeless people go."

Jesse-Ray walked to a nearby fast-food restaurant and ordered a biscuit, not yet knowing where his next stop would be. Before he'd eaten the biscuit, the friend came back with an answer: The Bluefield Union Mission in Bluefield, West Virginia.

The journey continued as the friend dropped him off at a bus stop outside a shopping center near Richlands, Virginia, about an hour's bus ride from Bluefield. Night had fallen so Jesse-Ray slept on the grass behind the largest store. The next morning, with only a few possessions and maybe thirty dollars in his fabric Bob Marley bag, he caught the bus, getting off at the Walmart in Bluefield, Virginia.

Walmart played a big part in the economic health of the adjoining towns that share a name—Bluefield, Virginia, and Bluefield, West Virginia. The towns are like Siamese twins. They share a border, and at many points, Virginia is on one side of the street, West Virginia on the other.

The Virginia Bluefield is much better off than the West Virginia Bluefield because of Walmart. The town government of Virginia Bluefield had welcomed Walmart. Not so the West Virginia Bluefield, which had snubbed the company's overtures. Having landed the big box store, the town coffers of Virginia Bluefield were full of Walmart's tax revenues—which funded municipal government, parks, and other amenities—while West Virginia Bluefield's town coffers were virtually empty of retail-related receipts. The latter town suffered and struggled and stagnated, its poorer residents visible night and day, walking up and down Bluefield Avenue. Jesse-Ray became one of them.

Although he knew no one in either Bluefield, Jesse-Ray was far from intimidated.

"I just started walking," Jesse-Ray said. "I am used to being homeless. I just started looking for houses." He shrugged, remembering. "Walked past some dude. Carrying all my shit."

The "dude" he noticed stood near a block of apartments. Street savvy, Jesse-Ray made a mental note about the place. Soon, some of the people living there would become his customers as he took up a familiar enterprise: dealing drugs.

He settled into life in Bluefield, staying mostly on the Virginia side of the state line, sleeping under a tree about a mile or two down the road from the Bluefield Union Mission, which was situated on the West Virginia side. After a couple of days, a man noticed Jesse-Ray's nighttime crib, grassy and out in the open. The stranger pointed out an abandoned house a couple of hundred yards back from the tree. Jesse-Ray explored the premises and found the property to his liking. There was no glass in the windows, and several of the walls were crumbling. But most of the roof was intact.

"Why didn't you go to Bluefield Union Mission right away?" I asked. "You came to town to change your life. After your friend found out about the mission from the police, getting there was your goal, right?"

"To be honest, I was too busy doing drugs."

"But you were out of money. How did you have money for drugs?"

Jesse-Ray laughed. He always seemed happiest when he knew something I didn't. "Simple drug dealer math," he said. "All you have to do is panhandle for a couple of hours to get fifty or sixty dollars." He outlined the formula: Put that initial money back into drugs, sell those drugs, turn the profit into more drugs. Repeat the cycle—staying clean yourself—until you have so much money that you possess enough drugs for continuing commerce. Then you can keep buying and selling with enough money and drugs left over to indulge yourself as well.

He stuck to his business plan until his transactions totaled $4,000 to $6,000 per shipment of marijuana at a time, with people from the apartments becoming his reliable, repeat customers. He settled into the abandoned house, walking everywhere, staying afloat financially even while high on drugs. He survived the winter; even, by some measures, thriving.

"I was the richest homeless guy in Bluefield," he said.

"If it was so great, why didn't you keep doing what you were doing? Why did you eventually go to the Bluefield Union Mission?"

Jesse-Ray took a deep breath. "I needed a place to turn my life around. I knew I was not going to turn my life around sitting in an abandoned house. I was so tired of living the same fucking thing every day.

"Walking sucks," he continued, warming to the subject. "Winter comes, and it's cold as fuck. I had to be high all the time. If I wasn't, I'd be freezing my balls off. So I smoked the last bit of my weed and thought, oh, fuck, I don't feel like walking four miles [to my supplier] and then walking around all day selling."

The moment of truth had arrived. He would either stay mired in a drug haze or ask for help.

Everyone for miles around knows the Bluefield Union Mission. It occupies a long block alongside a Dairy Queen, an auto parts store, a junk shop, and a convenience mart. Most of those buildings are a sorry sight, having been constructed years ago in Bluefield's better days. Across Bluefield Avenue sit the railroad tracks, where loads of coal and shipping containers traverse night and day, the train's engines so powerful they shake all the nearby buildings. An alley runs behind the mission, parallel to Bluefield Avenue and the railroad tracks. Perpendicular to the alley are short roads that run up the mountain, houses on either side—some brick, some clapboard—all built in the 1920s and many in disrepair. Looking at them, it is hard to imagine that Bluefield was once an affluent railroad town made rich by coal transport.

At first, Jesse-Ray stood outside the mission, the railroad tracks at his back, taking stock. The one-story building is smack on Bluefield Avenue, the main pedestrian drag for homeless people, drug users, prostitutes, and anyone else without a car. Three doors of the mission face the street, providing an entrance to the main dining hall as well as to the smaller office.

He noticed people going in and out one of the doors. He went inside. The door led into a small lobby with a closed door to the left, a tiny waiting room to the right, and an intake window immediately in front of him. Most days, a staff member sat on the other side of the window, which was opened for people to state their requests. Beyond the glass window was a main room furnished with computer desks. Bustling staff frequently moved throughout the large room, a central traffic area, which sometimes sported a conference table and other times was arranged with sofas and plush chairs, depending on what had been donated. Sometimes the staff, busy downstairs in the thrift shop or in the adjoining dining hall, were not in evidence. The day Jesse-Ray walked in, someone was there to hear his plea.

"Can I have food? Can I have a place to stay?"

As he told the story of that day, he seemed resentful at having to admit to other people how desperate he was. "Where the hell else was I going to get food and a place to stay?" he asked, reliving the moment.

As they did with virtually every hungry person who showed up, the mission staff gave him food. He returned the next day and the day after. Soon, they noticed how young and alone he was.

"He had nothing," one of the staff members told me later. "He had no one."

Meredith, the woman who would later become his supervisor at the mission, said that one cold day, Jesse-Ray showed up flushed and feverish. They invited him to lie down on a couch behind the counter until he felt better. They fed him, and they arranged for him to stay three nights at a local motel—three nights being the usual amount they would allocate someone in need of temporary lodging.

Jesse-Ray later confessed to me that he dealt drugs at the motel for the entire three days.

Rather than see him go back on the streets after his stint at the motel, the staff had a plan for Jesse-Ray. They told him he would be placed at the mission's new safe house: our place, where the paint was still drying on the walls.

Jesse-Ray was smart enough to know that sobriety would be expected. So how did he prepare for his transition into the safe house? By doing all the drugs he could get his hands on. He binged on pot and acid, vodka and whiskey. "I tried to get fucked up beyond belief," he said. "I knew it would be the last time."

From foster care to big-time drug dealing, from his dad's trailer to spending a winter outdoors—finally the picture seemed clearer about how and why he'd landed in Bluefield to pursue a different future.

"How does the world look to you sober?" I asked, trying to prompt him to reflect on his journey. "Can you give up the life you had? There's no more big money, like you had dealing drugs. Can you work hard for low pay and take incremental steps to improve your life? Live within a budget?"

He answered with a question, one of his rhetorical tactics. "Why not? Before, I would have just given in and sold drugs. But if I do that now, I know what would happen. It would fuck up everything I'm trying to do with my life."

But what *was* Jesse-Ray trying to do with his life? I noticed that Jesse-Ray's motivations were mostly framed in the negative. He didn't want to shiver in the cold. He didn't want to walk miles every day. He didn't want to stay mired in a boring life.

What I apparently chose to overlook was his lack of personal goals. I didn't want my perceptions clouded with evidence that Jesse-Ray might not live up to our expectations, so at the time, I blocked it from my sight. But in retrospect, Jesse-Ray rarely indicated that he saw a vision for his future. In our conversations or in his writing, he never imagined a moment that held a smiling Jesse-Ray in a graduation cap-and-gown or a mature Jesse-Ray with a career, a wife, and kids. In fact, he overtly rejected that scenario, hinting in an email that the work involved in creating a new life wasn't worth the payoff. He was trying to make it through each day, "but what for?" he asked. "Money? A better future? Maybe a wife and kids? Nah."

I tried to ignore that bald proclamation. I wasn't ready to consider that Jesse-Ray might not be on board with the idea of transformation—an idea that Hal and I cherished. In fact, even through late June and early July, when things began to fall apart, I was still clinging to illusions. Hal and I could envision Jesse-Ray becoming a different person, or at least the same person with a different life. Perhaps, the idealized picture in our minds was stronger than the actual Jesse-Ray who sat in front of us.

Abuse, neglect, and the educational plight of foster children

Here are numbers that suggest the size of the problem: Almost 400,000 children in America are in foster care; tragically, more than 1,500 children die from abuse or neglect each year. Nationally, more than 3 million children are the subject of a maltreatment report, with one-fifth of all reports confirming that the child is a victim of abuse or neglect.

Most victims are white (44 percent), Hispanic (22.7 percent) or African-American (21.4 percent). Almost 80 percent of the time when children are killed, the fatalities involve at least one parent.

In West Virginia, only after a policy change in 2014 did the state speed up first contact to require a response within 72 hours for reports of child abuse. The previous policy allowed two weeks to elapse before contact took place.

Studies have shown that foster children aged 16 or 17 who receive weekly coaching in "self-determination," along with instruction in setting goals and mentoring from former foster children, are more likely to graduate from high school or earn a GED degree (72 percent compared with 50 percent).

Sadly, less than 10 percent of children who've been in foster care graduate from college. Researchers at the Urban Institute argue that aged-out foster children will lack the credentials "needed to succeed in this economy without programs that can improve their educational outcomes and close the achievement gap." They recommend programs that help young people graduate from high school, improve their access to college, and help them succeed once enrolled.

By federal law since 2008, states may raise the age to which foster children are covered from 18 to 21. Currently, only a few states have adopted such a plan. Many teens see no advantage to staying in care. They voluntarily "age out" at 18 or after high school graduation, effectively cutting themselves off from money, resources, and advocates. They do so even though the odds are low of establishing a successful independent life without family or community support.

There are a number of places they can turn to for information and help. Local and national support-and-advocacy groups include:

- Child Welfare League of America
- Children's Bureau (a federal agency)
- The Children's Defense Fund
- National Foster Care Coalition
- Jim Casey Youth Opportunities Initiative
- National Resource Center for Permanency and Family Connections

CHAPTER 11

A spiritual vacuum

I have abandonment issues.
I have a quick temper.
I have a drug addiction.
I'm scared of the future.
I ask too many questions.

How do I change into something
that I don't know yet?

—Jesse-Ray Lewis, "Forgive Me"

It's no secret that the success of twelve-step groups is the acknowledgement of and reliance on a higher power. Sadly, no magic wand exists to obliterate addiction. But the twelve-step approach registers with many addicts, making it virtually the only proven treatment tool. Even doctor-run rehab centers incorporate twelve-step group work as a complement to medical interventions.

Hal's and my initial belief that Jesse-Ray could stay off drugs and get an education had seemed reasonable: Jesse-Ray exhibited pluck and smarts. It was conceivable that he could shift from the drug trade to a more legal, if less lucrative, line of work. Assuming that he could adopt a few new life skills, he was redeemable.

Hal and Craig and I had never sat down to formalize any kind of drug treatment program for Jesse-Ray, partly because we weren't professionally qualified to do so and partly because Jesse-Ray himself declared that he was clean and sober and wanted to stay that way.

But when we learned the extent of Jesse-Ray's drug problems, which dated to early childhood and included meth and other hard drugs, we realized that he probably needed residential rehab. I've seen residential rehab programs up close because I've had relatives committed to them, either voluntarily or by the courts. They typically involve twenty-four-hour camera surveillance, frequent drug tests, and a mandate that the client remain on the premises. Visitors are screened or disallowed entirely. Often, virtual lockdown is maintained for at least three months, a period deemed essential in the eyes of many addiction experts.

If Jesse-Ray had been admitted to residential treatment, twelve-step group participation with its spiritual component would have been part of the drill. The Bluefield Union Mission staff, along with Hal and me, explored independent lines of inquiry but could not find an inpatient program in West Virginia or Virginia that would accept Jesse-Ray, given his lack of ability to pay.

Further complicating matters, Jesse-Ray was adamant about not doing residential treatment. His resistance was expressed vehemently and often. Because treatment works only if the client is willing, we went along with this. Plus, we couldn't find an institution to take him.

The only practical form of treatment appeared to be the Narcotics Anonymous meetings that took place in downtown Bluefield, West Virginia. Hal and I hoped that Jesse-Ray would bond with a sponsor and invest himself in the introspective and humbling work of recovery.

Because of our own experiences with Al-Anon, the twelve-step program for friends and families of alcoholics, Hal and I knew that Jesse-Ray would be hearing about a higher power at his Narcotics Anonymous meetings five nights a week. Just like Alcoholics Anonymous and Narcotics Anonymous, Al-Anon stresses the need to surrender to a higher power as part of the healing process.

Because Hal and I both had close family members who'd struggled with addiction, we were familiar with the precepts of twelve-step programs.

The first step is to admit one's powerlessness over the addiction and to admit that one's life has become unmanageable; the second is to "believe that a power greater than ourselves could restore us to sanity." In 2013, while dealing with the continuing addiction problems of a close family member, I had met weekly with an Al-Anon sponsor for in-depth homework and study, the process called "working the steps." I delved even more deeply into the recovery process, confronting my own powerlessness over the situation and doing my best to maintain a sane and healthy outlook on life. I found that turning to a higher power was a vital step in achieving peace of mind. Sadly, after I reached step eight, which involves acknowledging how one has harmed others and considering ways to make amends, my sponsor was killed in an alcohol-related car crash. She was a young woman who attended Al-Anon meetings because she'd been raised by alcoholics. One night she drank too much and ran off the road. I was all too familiar with the devastation that drugs and alcohol can create and didn't have the heart to keep going to Al-Anon meetings. But I still believe wholeheartedly in the approach.

When Jesse-Ray shared his worries with Hal about how long he would be allowed to stay in the safe house, Hal tried to reassure him.

"You don't have to worry about food or shelter," Hal said. "You can stay as long as you keep up with the program."

The so-called makeshift "program" was simple—he had to practice good hygiene, get ready for college, pick up after himself, attend Narcotics Anonymous meetings, volunteer at the mission, and participate in the spiritual instruction of his choosing. Hal and I believed that a spiritual component was an essential part of his shaking free from drug addiction and the lure of gangs.

After Hal had asked Jesse-Ray if he believed in God, Jesse-Ray had shot back, "Would I be here if I didn't?" Later, I had followed up with Jesse-Ray, asking if he'd been honest with Hal in implying that he was a believer. The answer was that Jesse-Ray didn't have much use for God.

"God had his chance, and God already did a number on me," he told me. He said that he wondered where God was—if there was such a thing—when he was being mistreated as a child. He was familiar with the Old Testament version of God, wrathful and punishing. His own father had punished him enough; why would he want to let God—just another bully—into his life? Surrender made no sense to Jesse-Ray, and he declined to submit to a "higher power," regardless of it being a central tenet of the Narcotics Anonymous approach. Even though Hal didn't attend the meetings with him, he sensed that Jesse-Ray was holding back. He accused him of a stubborn refusal to submit, which Jesse-Ray freely acknowledged.

His resistance surprised and disappointed us because we wanted Jesse-Ray to open himself to healing concepts. We feared that his rejection of the central proposition of the twelve-step program would jeopardize his chances of conquering addiction. When he had first showed up on our doorstep, Jesse-Ray had seemed wide-eyed and willing to change. He had said that he wanted nothing more to do with drugs. We wanted to believe him, but maybe he was just adept at saying what people wanted to hear.

The last thing Hal and I intended to do was force a belief system on Jesse-Ray. At nineteen years old, he was legally an adult. At the same time, we felt obligated to cobble together a drug-recovery regimen with a chance of success. There was no sense having Jesse-Ray in the safe house unless he was on the road to a productive future. And because we knew that a spiritual component was vital to his recovery, it was unthinkable to leave spirituality out of the equation.

Even though Jesse-Ray seemed wholly mired in materialistic thinking—his focus was uniformly fixed on acquiring money and goods—we believed that his state of consciousness had to change.

He'd already survived brushes with death. The odds were stacked against his survival. Downward-spiraling drug addicts typically don't enjoy long lifespans.

He was someone who'd done bad things but who still possessed a conscience. The negative thoughts that often consumed him included guilt over past misdeeds. But he could be kind. During one of our weekend chats, he told me a story about a younger boy who came out to him as gay. Fearful and uncertain, the boy—the younger brother of the kid who'd put marijuana on Jesse-Ray's bed—still hadn't told his parents. Jesse-Ray assured him that his sexual orientation didn't matter. Everything was okay, he told the younger boy. He still viewed him the same. I was glad to know that even though his own life was difficult, he could still exhibit compassion for others.

Hal and I set about working to broaden Jesse-Ray's concepts of God, to introduce elements of love and wonder and creation and joy into his life. We didn't dictate the form that his spiritual explorations might take. We started by exposing him to my church, suggesting that he choose between church attendance and individual Bible study with Hal.

Hal and I are of different denominations. Hal's denomination doesn't have a church in our small town so, for the first month or two, Jesse-Ray went to church with me. My church is tiny, with about eight people on hand most Sundays. Aside from some hymn-singing, things are staid. Readings in this metaphysically oriented Christian church make up most of the service. A couple of times during his first experience sitting in the pew, Jesse-Ray almost nodded off to the droning background of the first and second readers standing side by side at the lecterns.

Toward the end of the service, one of the members brought around the collection basket. When I put money into it, Jesse-Ray cut me a look out of the corner of his eyes.

"Do you have to pay to go to church?"

"No. It's a voluntary donation."

He reared back in the pew, reacting with stunned disbelief. Out of earshot of the others, he pronounced church "boring," even though the ideas that had been articulated during the service were radical, defining evil as an unreal concept and describing man's true identity as wholly spiritual. Apparently, none of it registered with Jesse-Ray.

After the hour was up, the church members gathered in the lobby, lingering to chat. Naturally, they were curious about him, and Jesse-Ray sensed an audience. His pent-up energy and awkwardness came out as he almost seemed to career from one point to another, shifting his weight from leg to leg, standing first on one side of the group before moving elsewhere. He seemed to be holding court.

People introduced themselves, and Jesse-Ray learned that four of the congregants were related—middle-aged brother and sister, elderly mother and aunt. Jesse-Ray remarked that it must be like a family reunion for them, coming to church.

"A family reunion would never happen to me at a church," he said, drawing out the syllables in his Appalachian drawl. He waited a comedic beat, then followed with the punchline, "Maybe at a jail."

He grinned, regaling the congregation with his outrageous talk. But many of these Christian Scientists were lifelong educators. All of them were down to earth. None was scandalized.

Unable to stand still, he lurched across the church lobby, filled with exuberant energy that didn't seem fully within his control. Jesse-Ray loved the limelight.

"I've been told that if I ever set foot in a church, I would spontaneously combust."

The retired principal in the group smiled. "You'd be good in the theater," he said, knowing how to gentle along an unruly teen.

"They said a Bible would go up in flames if I touched it," Jesse-Ray declared.

Everyone laughed. The congregation was friendly and welcoming. They seemed to find his blasphemous innocence charming.

He suggested to me later that his showing up at my church was probably the high point of the congregants' week, given that they were old and lived boring lives. He often played the clownish juvenile, and his high spirits didn't end at the sanctuary door.

One of the church members was a professor of English at a nearby college. After Jesse-Ray had come to church once or twice, she offered to tutor him one-on-one in the basement classroom during the service. In Christian Science, Sunday School covers young people up to age twenty, so Jesse-Ray could have had almost a whole year of private instruction if he desired. I was thrilled with her offer because, as a professor, she was another role model for him in the world of literature. She had read some of his poetry and concurred with my opinion of his talent.

I discussed her offer with Jesse-Ray. Before agreeing to Sunday School, he asked, "She won't laugh at me, will she?" Despite his cutups in the lobby, he was worried about appearing stupid.

He agreed to the sessions, which seemed to be good for both of them. The professor complimented him on his reading comprehension and writing flair. In the classroom, she introduced him to the novel concept of his wholly spiritual, true identity. Far from laughing at his ignorance, she remarked on how keen and insightful his questions were.

But the arrangement didn't last. Jesse-Ray wasn't impressed. After a couple of weeks, Jesse-Ray made it plain that he had no appetite for getting cleaned up and dressed for Sunday School, even in a church that viewed him not as a wretch or a hopeless loser but as the ever-perfect reflection of God.

He exercised the option of choice, saying he'd prefer to do Bible study with Hal.

As his spiritual instruction shifted to Hal, Jesse-Ray couldn't have known what he was in for. Hal has a deep knowledge of the Bible. He's passionate about the spiritual principles the ancient text articulates. And he was raised in a triumphalist church—a church that believes its way is the only right and true path to God.

Hal took the responsibility to heart. True to form, he was an exacting taskmaster. He tried to reach Jesse-Ray in various ways, holding up and highlighting Bible passages that might apply to Jesse-Ray's life. They dove into the story of the prodigal son, in which the son violates all the rules, leaves home for a time of riotous living and, despite his sins, is fully embraced by his father upon his return. It seemed like a Bible story tailor-made for Jesse-Ray. But the first Sunday was a disaster, and the second not much better. Jesse-Ray was polite but disaffected. He didn't connect with the biblical language. He wasn't getting it. He sat there yawning, not even feigning interest.

I urged Hal to try something different because dry reading exercises were not going to cut it for Jesse-Ray. That's when Hal got the idea of taking Jesse-Ray on a walk up our mountain so that Jesse-Ray could observe the hand of nature, large and small.

"Our mountain" extends from our stone-terraced yard up through the woods. Hal and I often walk up the steep ascent together, wearing shoes with cleats and carrying walking sticks to dig into the hillside for balance. There are no paths except the narrow game trails carved into the mountainside by small herds of deer. Ten minutes of steady trekking among oak, pine, locust and tulip trees brings you to a ridge where, winded, you can stand and take in a 360-degree panorama of mountaintops.

Having been out in the woods with Hal on photo shoots, I've often admired how he could spot animals camouflaged in the underbrush, hundreds of yards away, or identify how a tree has responded to a lightning strike or twisted itself against the invasion of a bigger tree. Even the tiniest of flowers don't escape his notice. Maybe it's because he learned so much from the shamans in the jungles of Panama where he grew up. Or maybe he's just a preternaturally observant person. At any rate, Hal could step outside the back door and become instantly attuned to the life pulsating around him.

On their walk, Hal and Jesse-Ray gazed at the vast shimmering mountain ridge in the distance. They peered through a magnifying glass at the tiny white flowers sprinkled throughout the moss. They looked at flowers and bugs, Hal pointing out shapes and colors that inspired marvel. Jesse-Ray seemed grateful for the interlude.

"I didn't realize there were all these differences you couldn't see with the naked eye," Jesse-Ray told me later. Whether he connected the appreciation of nature with the spiritual vision Hal intended to convey was another matter.

Later, as I tried to foster Jesse-Ray's development as a writer, I asked him to recall that mountain walk. "You took a close look at the tiny flowers to observe them, remember? You told Hal that was a completely new experience for you. And Hal told me you both saw a rainbow that day. How did it feel, seeing that rainbow? Write it!"

He never did.

From our perspective, additional spiritual activities and exercises were optional. But we encouraged them nonetheless, hoping new, positive thought patterns would emerge. For instance, I suggested that, each night, he write down three things he was grateful for, then share these with me at the end of the week. He didn't.

Yet Hal and I were not entirely without influence. Sometimes Jesse-Ray articulated surprising new views of himself and his life. Once he said that he sometimes woke up thinking that he was happy to be alive.

He professed to make progress on other fronts as well.

"I'm trying to build something," Jesse-Ray told me as evidence of his commitment to our program of rehabilitation. "This time, I'm trying my best to have a life where I'm not fucked up all the time."

"Do you have a goal?"

"I'm working to get to a place where my mind isn't filled with thoughts that are bad for me and others."

"What about the future?" I asking, knowing it was a question he preferred not to address.

"I get anxious when I think too far ahead," he said. "What I am thinking about is the next ten minutes."

During this phase—after the jail stay and while Jesse-Ray was still sitting through Hal's weekly Bible-study lessons—Jesse-Ray seemed to be taking two steps forward, one step back. One of the forward steps occurred on a Sunday, when he wore a blue shirt that I had bought him, despite the fact that he hated the color. I hadn't even noticed that the shirt was blue when I purchased it. I was touched when Hal called me in Blacksburg and told me that Jesse-Ray had said he'd worn the shirt for me; I was the only person he'd wear blue for. He'd taken a step outside his comfort zone.

We didn't expect perfection. But Jesse-Ray had come to Bluefield looking to change his life—or so we thought. Hal gave him total commitment as a mentor, confidant, and advocate. He spent hours each evening on the Internet, looking for ways to make Jesse-Ray's drug withdrawal easier. He made sure Jesse-Ray had good food to eat (cooking for him when Jesse-Ray's larder was bare), plenty of sleep, and step-by-step instructions on how to overcome any daily obstacle that might come up.

Even as Hal did more for Jesse-Ray, Jesse-Ray seemed to do less for himself. Hal and I suggested many objectives he could be accomplishing, such as reading books to prepare for college or learning the Bluefield bus system so that he could easily travel to Princeton when classes began. Jesse-Ray did none of it. He wasn't even living up to his daily obligations. He didn't take the trash to the curb on Tuesday mornings. Didn't get up on time. Didn't budget his food-stamp money, blowing it all on junk food by the middle of the month. Didn't follow Hal's advice to make himself valued at the Bluefield Union Mission by doing extra tasks such as picking up trash around the grounds.

Had Hal become an enabler? Was he contributing to Jesse-Ray's problems by stepping in to solve them, sparing him the consequences of his own behavior?

"You can't want Jesse-Ray's recovery more than he wants it

himself," I said, not wanting to be overbearing but not liking what I was witnessing.

Hal, a doer and a giver, found it tough to change. He didn't see the line between "doing" and "enabling." And yet, even Hal grew frustrated with Jesse-Ray's lack of effort.

To keep Hal's rescue instincts in check, we came up with a three-part test to help decide when he would step in. Hal liked it so much that, just as he posted cleanup rules in Jesse-Ray's kitchen for Jesse-Ray, he posted the guidelines in his own kitchen for himself:

1. Don't do anything for Jesse-Ray that he can reasonably be expected to do for himself.

2. Don't spare him the consequences of any of his bad behavior (mouthing off at the mission, spending all his food stamp money, etc.).

3. Don't agree to any of his requests that would turn your own life upside down.

For months, we clung to our idea of Jesse-Ray as a young man who only needed someone to believe in him. We were certain that he would benefit from a measured understanding of things hallowed or holy, the cultivation of a sense of gratitude, and perhaps even lift his gaze above himself to thoughts of a higher power. I believed this even though he wrote in an email that there was "not much touch of higher being in me."

For a time, Hal's weekly Bible-study lessons were a vital element of the recovery "program." But Jesse-Ray didn't embrace them; he simply endured them. Soon we began to wonder whether the spiritual vacuum was something Jesse-Ray would remain loath to fill.

Higher powers

Bill Wilson, the founder of Alcoholics Anonymous, experienced an existential crisis while in a hospital recovering from what would be his last drinking binge.

"I still gagged badly on the notion of a Power greater than myself, but finally, just for the moment, the last vestige of my proud obstinacy was crushed," Wilson wrote.

He begged for God, if such a thing existed, to reveal itself. A flash of white light and a feeling of ecstasy arose within himself, along with the conviction that he had attained overwhelming peace and well-being—in short, the Presence.

"It seemed to me, in my mind's eye, that I was on a mountain and that a wind not of air but of spirit was blowing," said Wilson. "And then it burst upon me that I was a free man."

Though Alcoholics Anonymous is famously nondenominational, the role of spirituality in twelve-step programs cannot be overstated. "God" as a circumscribed concept is not forced on people. But the concept of surrender to a higher power is pre-eminent. The higher-power focus may have put Alcoholics Anonymous, Narcotics Anonymous, and other such programs on the fringes of scientific respectability, but at the same time, many medical doctors and recovery experts point to twelve-step programs as the best-known means to achieve long-term sobriety.

Paul Gallant, a New York-based interventionist with more than two decades of sobriety, says that psychotherapy and other forms of analysis, such as self-knowledge, don't necessarily evoke the "spiritual awakening" that leads to profound behavioral transformation.

"The not-drinking is really just a part of it," he explained. "That psychic change needs to come from a program of spiritual development, and so far, the greatest success has been Alcoholics Anonymous."

Scientific research continues to associate spiritual and religious experiences with the brain's complex neural networks. A 2016 study involving brain scans of young adult Mormons corroborated previous research that prayer and meditation practices achieved "changes in the attentional areas of the brain and also the striatum," according to Andrew Newberg, a pioneer in neurotheology and professor of emergency medicine and radiology at Thomas Jefferson University.

In a National Public Radio discussion of addiction, Marvin Seppala, chief medical officer of the merged Hazelden-Betty Ford Center, said, "This is a disease not just of the brain, but also of the soul." Elaborating in a question-and-answer session with TheFix.com, he commented on the irony of the fields of psychology and psychiatry almost entirely omitting mindfulness and spiritual practices from their disciplines.

Both psychology and psychiatry are fixated on "a pathological approach," Seppala said. One would think those fields would make spiritual practices "an inherent part of the general examination of a person's health and psyche." But they don't. "There's a void," he states. "Although there is starting to be a shift towards recognizing the importance of the positive emotions, it still does not enter into the major textbooks and has not been incorporated into the educational normative for most psychologists and psychiatrists."

English comedian and actor Russell Brand, who went public with his addiction to sex and drugs, is the author of *Recovery: Freedom from Our Addictions*. In an exchange with marijuana aficionado Bill Maher on HBO's Real Time, Brand reflected:

"For me, the only drug that I'm interested in is the drug that we are pursuing in the first place: the drug of connection, of unity, of love. For me, all these things are placeboes—every drug, every commodity, just a placeholder on the way—false idols, as we seek out some kind of truth and connection, in whatever denomination, in whatever language, whether it's agnostically, atheistically, or religiously. We're all looking for oneness."

CHAPTER 12

Writing to a beat

Bodies on the floor.
Loved ones dead
or comatose
self-inflicted overdose.

Today I'm a young man
trying to pass an entrance exam
breaking up those memories with every word
I write.

—Jesse-Ray Lewis, "Turning Point"

In an attempt to celebrate his potential, Hal and I offered encouragement to Jesse-Ray wherever we could. He had barely made it out of high school, but he was bright. At times he was self-centered and almost surly, but he became energized when people paid attention to him, and his personality would sparkle.

His writing talent was a gift we could capitalize on. Even though his writing efforts produced rhymes that were rough and unpunctuated, they harbored fresh phrasing and curiously apt metaphors. He had the makings of a writer who could support himself with his craft. His unfortunate and sometimes violent past gave him much to write about, with his singular take on life originating as much from his Appalachian roots as his youth.

We did our best to cheer him on. We tried to make each goal

attainable. We broke down large tasks into simple steps, such as the approach to college. First, he submitted the application, then he took the placement tests, then he studied the multiplication tables before retaking the tests, and so forth. But no matter how supportive we were, or how simple the next objective, he disparaged every prediction we made about his potential and clung to his sense of self as someone who lived in society's underbelly and probably always would.

"You say I'm this great writer," he seethed, lifting his arms in an exaggerated gesture to convey his disbelief.

"I'm saying nothing of the sort," I retorted. "I'm saying you could be a great writer if you worked hard."

It was always a balancing act, encouraging him to celebrate his talent while at the same time stressing that most goals worth achieving required persistence. Thinking I could convince him of the power of effort, I told him one of my favorite quotes, from Thomas Edison: "Genius is one percent inspiration, ninety-nine percent perspiration." At this junction, I knew better than to tell him how tough and lonely the writing life can be. I was waiting until he had more experience to spring on him another classic quote authors love to share: "Writing is easy. You just open a vein and bleed."

Jesse-Ray had a history as a writer. As a child, he'd kept journals, which I viewed as confirmation that his hobby might become his vocation. I wished I could read them, but the journals were no longer in his possession. I could only imagine him as a perceptive child, witnessing death and violence, abandonment and addiction, and trying to make sense of it. Jesse-Ray said the journals were out of reach, at his father's place. I suggested that we try to contact his father, but Jesse-Ray claimed that his father prized the journals. "He'll never give them up," he said. Reluctantly, I dropped the idea, but I didn't stop thinking about it.

"It's the only thing that kept me from going crazy," he said of his journaling. For him, writing verse was a way to vent his emotions and mentally process his childhood trauma. He once told me in an email that pen and paper were a way of understanding his own thoughts. He followed this with a rare glimpse of self-awareness: "I fought all my life to survive tied up with chains I made myself."

I might have been kidding myself, but I believed that Jesse-Ray was beginning to see where his writing gifts could take him. Still referring to the chains that bound him, he wrote that he was breaking through them with every word. "My burdens not only get lifted, they take flight far away from the cavern of thoughts that is my mind." For Jesse-Ray, writing was a creative and liberating act, and for me, encouraging his gift seemed like a way to break his imprisonment in a whirl of negative thoughts.

Jesse-Ray, still disbelieving that readers might like his poems, had an eye-opening experience toward the end of April when Hal and I escorted him to a writers' gathering in Roanoke, Virginia. In front of an audience of more than a dozen people, he read one of his longer poems. The experienced writers and lyricists who made up the crowd were appreciative of his work. Many approached him afterward. "Keep writing!" one of them encouraged him.

After we began compiling poems that I knew would be strong enough to fill a chapbook, I promised to look for an agent or a publisher for *Hillbilly Drug Baby: The Poems*. Jesse-Ray was skeptical that anyone would want to publish them. But he seemed to enjoy the magic of his phrases being sculpted and broken into lines that showed off their rhythms. Unlike some amateur writers, he did not resent editing. My editing often consisted of throwing away two thirds of what he wrote and stringing together the remaining diamonds.

As I edited Jesse-Ray's work, I kept in mind the Michelangelo anecdote about artistry. When asked how he crafted the masterpiece, the sculptor replied, "It's simple. I just removed everything from the stone that was not David."

Jesse-Ray loved the artful line breaks that spun his phrases out on the page. He loved the look of poems. He was thrilled when his favorite book, *Crank*, was donated to the Bluefield Union Mission.

He bought the book for a few pennies and lent it to me. To me, this demonstrated that Jesse-Ray, who didn't respect much, respected the reach of poetry. Knowing his reverence for the work of someone of Ellen Hopkins' stature intensified my desire to cultivate his talents. He appreciated powerful prose and poetry and could aspire to create it.

His drafts could be incoherent. They came in streams of consciousness, full of misspellings and mispunctuation. A casual reader might have dismissed his phrases as gibberish. Many of the lines were clichéd and infused with sentimentality. To him, writing had always been a form of therapy, so he never thought about polishing his work for readers. He once told me, "When I write, there's this peacefulness. I can get transported to a different world—a world that has no stress." But I saw art in his originality. He had a knack for creating audacious images, painting events with authenticity, exposing a soul that wanted to rise and roar.

I worried that, after his poems were published, someone might interview Jesse-Ray or review a piece of his unedited writing and declare him a fraud and me a puppet master. I fretted that his writing wouldn't be judged on its merits, that reviewers or journalists might say he couldn't produce poetry without a ghostwriter propping him up.

But I can attest that the words are Jesse-Ray's, not mine. Adding a transitional phrase here or there didn't take away his authorship. I came to believe that, in the tradition of American publishing, I'd discovered a talented young man sprung from unfortunate circumstances—if not a prodigy. Jesse-Ray might have been a semi-literate child who'd been labeled a crack baby, but he was also a poet whose words could move readers.

When Jesse-Ray readied himself to write, he put on music—a beat, he called it—the wordless music allowing him to spin out prose in rap-like cadences. His emails arrived with words run together with no attempt to spell or punctuate correctly. But they were full of conflict and heart, like when he "had to fight just to eat" and was forced to "give my bloodstained heart away to a demon scheming on how he is going to fuck me over." He grew "tired of fighting, crawling naked on broken glass."

With equal dolor, Jesse-Ray bleakly observed that on government and institutional forms, "they ask for next-of-kin, but I have none." But he could also be wry: "I sold drugs to my dad, thinking, *'I'm making money!'* But later I found out he was paying me with money he got from the government for me." Sometimes his words exuded a hint of resolute resilience, and his ability to juxtapose emotions further signaled his potential as an author. Some of Jesse-Ray's lines gave me goosebumps ("They spit on the grave of a lost boy") and others tiptoed to the edge of being overwrought ("I find a single droplet of hope and choke on it"). I felt like a Tiger Mom, not wanting anyone to take an iota of credit away from him. His talent was real, and at times it awed me.

Hal and I yearned to fix Jesse-Ray's life. We didn't know if we could succeed. But I knew that as a veteran editor, I could bring his writing to publishable standards. Every time I finished editing a poem, I marveled at his ability to craft imagery, to evoke sights and smells, to make startling comparisons.

To further expose him to writing professionals, I registered him in the Southern Appalachian Heritage Writers Symposium in Richlands, Virginia, in early June. Coincidentally, Richlands is where he'd spent his first homeless night, sleeping in the grass outside the big box store, waiting to take the morning bus to Bluefield.

Conference organizers at Southwest Virginia Community College were kind enough to waive his registration fee for the two-day event. On the first day of the conference, a Friday, Hal dropped work to take Jesse-Ray to the college, which was forty-five minutes away. The second day, I planned to go to the workshops with him, hoping to start a dialogue between him and the other writers.

I was up and out the door early on Saturday morning, knowing that Hal had instructed Jesse-Ray to be ready by 8 a.m. I drove the few feet to the safe house driveway. No Jesse-Ray. Hal knocked on his door. As the minutes passed, I wasn't even sure if Jesse-Ray was awake. Jesse-Ray emerged after a few minutes, looking rumpled in a long-sleeved shirt. But at least he was clean and presentable.

Unapologetic for being late, Jesse-Ray had an immediate request. We had just pulled onto Bluefield Avenue when he motioned toward the convenience mart. Again, I idled for a few minutes before he emerged with an energy drink full of caffeine and sugar, along with some sort of processed white-flour item he called breakfast.

I later asked Hal why he didn't counsel Jesse-Ray to stock up on food. Hal replied that he'd talked to Jesse-Ray about the concept to no avail. Jesse-Ray never planned and never shopped ahead. He spent most of his food-stamp money on junk food from the convenience mart.

The morning's keynote speak was Saundra Kelley, author of the story collection *The Day the Mirror Cried*, so I didn't want to be late. But Jesse-Ray's tardiness and the breakfast stop made that an impossible goal. Kelley is a writer I've known for more than twenty years and a keen observer of people. She later shared her impressions of Jesse-Ray as we walked into her presentation ten minutes late.

"He had a look that was one step up from homeless, and it was definitely true to type—heavy, out-of-season flannel shirt, thick dark baggy jeans," she said. "He was handsome in a rough way."

After she had the chance to talk with him, she found him likable. "I sensed two controversial things about him: resistance and a desire to please," she told me later. "He missed very little in that room of Appalachian writers but I think he was uncomfortable." She further noticed that he kept an eye out for my presence, taking care to know where I was at all times.

The conference took place in a new, cavernous building filled with classrooms, all cast in neutral colors with plenty of natural light pouring in through giant windows. The day before, Hal had reported that the environment had seemed to intimidate Jesse-

Ray. He noticed that Jesse-Ray seemed in awe, craning his neck to view the expanse of the two-story atrium. But at the same time, Jesse-Ray was able to settle in, remarking to Hal, "So this is what community college is like?" Hal interpreted his tone to mean that Jesse-Ray could see himself functioning in college in neighboring West Virginia when fall semester started in a couple of months.

Jesse-Ray sat quietly through Kelley's storytelling talk. Afterwards, another high-profile speaker took the podium. Five minutes into the man's talk, I could feel Jesse-Ray mentally withdraw. He stared down at his own pen and paper, then began to write, giving up all pretense of paying attention. His disengagement disappointed me, because I thought he could glean much from the speaker, the mega-bestselling author Scott Pratt, who'd grown up in poverty and become a writer despite much adversity.

Later I asked Jesse-Ray why he'd turned away. He said that he'd been outraged by something Pratt had said. Pratt, a US Air Force veteran and author of legal thrillers, had carefully outlined the reason for the occasionally irrational, self-destructive actions of the main character of his novel, a lawyer. They stemmed from the fact that his sister had been raped as a child.

"Who would trade on such a terrible thing to entertain people and make money?" Jesse-Ray snorted in disgust.

"He's trying to explain that what happened to the lawyer's sister leads the lawyer to make mistakes and to do crazy things, when in fact he's only trying to see justice done," I explained. "He's giving his characters human flaws and motivations. As a writer you need to understand that."

Jesse-Ray wasn't mollified. While he was content to practice decorum through the conference's hour-long workshops, stealing out only for occasional smoke breaks, he didn't ask any questions during the Q&A periods. Nor did he seem curious about any of the writers or their challenges or successes.

The one moment he seemed fully inspired came when several of the conference speakers set up stacks of their books on tables to offer their works for sale. Buyers were scarce, as the rural college's buildings had no foot traffic, especially on a Saturday. The only people buying books were the conference goers themselves. The atmosphere was sedate, almost stale. Few transactions were taking place.

Jesse-Ray sprang into action. He took it upon himself to hawk Kelley's books as she sat behind her table. He loved an audience, and her goal of moving merchandise gave him an opportunity to shine. Having proved himself a skilled salesman in the drug trade, he demonstrated his sales prowess to us. I also suspected he was more comfortable talking than listening; he would have gotten more out of the conference by engaging with some of the assembled authors. But listening wasn't his style.

He accosted people in the hallways, herding them to Kelley and her piles of books for sale, which included a book of tall tales as well as a book of interviews with Appalachian storytellers. He helped move four or five books by rounding up unsuspecting buyers, talking up what a great writer she was. Of course, this was something he had no way of knowing, having never read any of her books.

Toward the end of the day, when Jesse-Ray was outside smoking, Kelley said of his hucksterism, "I was amazed at the comfort level he presented. I say that because I'm not entirely certain it was completely real." She wondered if he was adopting a persona to feel more purposeful, legitimate, and secure. I agreed that he was.

"And he really was working just as he probably does on the streets," she added. "Trained properly, he could be a marketing powerhouse or a deadly salesman."

As we drove home, Jesse-Ray boasted, "It's easy to sell books."

"Hold that thought," I retorted. "We'll see how many books you sell next year when your poetry comes out."

Shortly before the conference, Hal and Jesse-Ray and I had celebrated the acceptance of his poetry for publication. A few remaining poems still needed to be composed to flesh out the chapbook. But the publisher, based in Christiansburg, Virginia—

not far from the university where I worked—had liked what I'd shown her, and she had made an on-the-spot acceptance. She provided a multipage contract for Jesse-Ray, which I brought home to Bluefield for Jesse-Ray to sign. Hal and I were ecstatic. *Hillbilly Drug Baby: The Poems* was going to be a reality! As he initialed and signed the contract, I remarked to Jesse-Ray that he seemed blasé.

"Doesn't this mean anything to you?" I asked. "Do you know how many writers would kill to be accepted by a publishing house, to become a published author?"

"Yeah," he answered. "But I never really get excited about anything."

Less than sixty days after the conference, Jesse-Ray was gone from our lives.

After the conference, I asked Saundra Kelley, who had read his poetry before meeting him, to think back to her impressions of Jesse-Ray, including the hour we'd sat together during the luncheon. Kelley is a generous, forgiving soul and a good judge of character. I wanted to see Jesse-Ray through her eyes. She knew how hard Hal and I had labored, trying to help him build a productive life, and I wondered if I had missed something essential about him along the way. I was shocked when she said she had instantly pegged him as a "taker."

"What makes you say that?" I could hear the incredulity in my own voice. I had never recognized that side of him.

"When I met him at the conference, he'd pretty much figured out how far to push you two and still get a meal and a safe place to sleep," she replied. "The way he misused the privilege, with an arrogance that I still find amazing, shows that he believed he could take everything you offered, and if he gave just enough in return, you'd keep fussing over him and trying to help. More bad judgment on his part."

Finishing her unsparing assessment, she added a comment about the environment from which he sprang:

"He's the product of an upbringing from hell, an alternate drug culture seething just below the surface all over the country, this one wearing the face of Appalachia. It was one he didn't know how to overcome, and neither did you and Hal."

Her words sobered me, because Kelley knew, far better than I did, how growing up in a backwoods environment could shape a person. She herself was a fifth-generation north Floridian who'd sprung from the swampy, forested rural regions of the state, and while her parents were good providers, she also lived in close proximity to families not so different from Jesse-Ray's.

Looking back at my time with Jesse-Ray, it's his promise as a writer I sorrow over most. I regret the missed opportunities.

In addition to overseeing his chapbook of poems, I also wanted to give him one-on-one instruction. I wanted to show him why some of his lines worked and why others were axed. I wanted to train him to spot sentimentality and cliché in his first drafts so that he could write more polished second and third drafts.

I wanted to teach him the basics of rhyme and meter and the wild freedom of poetic language. I wanted to influence him to augment his lexicon of blood and violence with at least some vocabulary of beauty and hope.

I even went so far as to scour the Internet for the long out-of-print *Discovery of Poetry* written by my own beloved teacher, the late Thomas E. Sanders, a published author and poet who taught for many years at the University of South Florida in Tampa. The book arrived by mail just days before Jesse-Ray's exit, leaving no time for tutoring.

I'm still angry when I think about it. Jesse-Ray was possessed of talent and had an eye for detail. He wrote with honesty and an edge. He knew how to plumb his brutal past for material. With training, he could have parlayed his singular voice into a writing career. He could have written his way out of poverty, one choice word at a time.

Did he choose not to hone his skills? Or was he never interested from the start? Maybe one day he'll write again, and I'll get answers.

When poetry becomes a liberator

Poetry and rap have provided lifelines for disaffected youth in America for decades, their words and works bubbling with scathing critiques of their worlds.

In the early days, the literary output of teens was not valued or acknowledged in schools, according to research about the power of teenage rap.

In rap and raw poetry, teens meet issues head-on, including poverty, violence, crime, and drugs. They take refuge in the free, rough creativity the genres provide.

Today rap is mainstream, with poetry slams a staple in every big city, not to mention churches and other entities devoted to spiritual healing that have embraced the art form.

"Pray 4 My Hood" was a music video and the theme of a 2015 tour targeting more than sixty cities by Christian rapper Sevin, formerly a gang member in California and a twelve-year veteran of homelessness. The block parties were designed to hit "the most unreached neighborhoods in America" with the offer of "hope and love in the midst of darkness."

The Rev. Victor Moore, a hip-hop artist himself, brought Sevin's tour to Canton, Ohio, in September 2017, saying, "I thought it would be a good idea to bring some love and ministry to this community by having these artists come and just do what they do."

With lyrics such as "It's a war zone out here," and "Straight shot toddler hit/Leakin' while he twitch and scream," Sevin's artistic expression is eerily reminiscent of Jesse-Ray's. But in sharp contrast to Jesse-Ray, who stayed stuck in his torment, the Christian rapper was able to pivot toward faith, hope, and love. He has found his way to the truth of Martin Luther King's pronouncement, working an audio recording of the impassioned words of King's into his song: "And a man has not begun to live until he can rise above the narrow confines of his own individual concerns to the broader concerns of all humanity."

"When young people write or engage in spoken-word poetry, they can achieve a measure of healing," says Wendy Williams, an Arizona State University professor who studies how young people benefit by writing. "There are connections between rap and poetry—the rhythms and use of rhyme. A lot of people do both, and both spoken-word and rap are part of hip-hop culture . . . In some cases, these kids are writing about abuse and difficult experiences. It's great because they're finding an emotional release."

Through his verse, Jesse-Ray may have taken on the roles of "source," "investigator," and "archiver" of a rich body of knowledge rooted in the cultural and linguistic world from which he sprang—the three roles identified by researchers who study so-called out-of-school writing. Sadly, he has not yet progressed to the point of finding complete healing through his writing, despite his originality, talent, and willingness to confront truth.

CHAPTER 13

The screw-ups begin

My mind tells me:
If you just slip back
you will be fine.
— Jesse-Ray Lewis, "Depression"

In one of our early conversations, Jesse-Ray came up with a metaphor to convey how being a foster kid felt like being adrift in the world.

"When you're building Legos, you have to have something to build the Legos on—a foundation, the ground," he said. "We foster kids don't have anything. We have air."

With an understanding of the deficits that underpinned Jesse-Ray's early life, compassionate, loving Hal became his mentor, anchor, and friend. Hal hoped that consistently playing those roles would be enough to shore Jesse-Ray up.

Navigating the bureaucracy entailed multiple trips to Princeton, the county seat. Even the process of transferring Jesse-Ray's foster-care case to West Virginia (he'd aged out of foster care in Virginia) was complicated. Many meetings, phone calls, in-person visits, and online applications were required to set Jesse-Ray up with services, including medical benefits. Jesse-Ray could not handle any of it by himself. Hand-holding was a major part of Hal's job description.

When Hal and I talked on the phone at night, I'd hear about events such as when Jesse-Ray would see a policeman and say something angry or condemning. Hal would try to reason with him.

He'd talk about how police were just doing their jobs, sometimes laying their lives on the line to protect people like us. From time to time, Jesse-Ray seemed to accept that a perspective other than his might be valid. But in the next breath, he'd argue that the police were staring at him.

"They look at me like I'm a criminal when I walk down the street," Jesse-Ray said.

"You look like every other drug dealer around here," Hal pointed out. "You walk with a slouch, your cuffs are dragging on the ground, and your pants are falling down, and everyone can see your butt crack. You fit the profile."

Hal bought him a belt and urged Jesse-Ray to keep it tightened. Even that simple step, over time, became a losing battle.

Sometimes Jesse-Ray would show progress in adopting a more mature outlook. When it came to manners, he followed Hal's lead. For instance, even if a government office couldn't give them what they'd come for, Hal would always stand up at the end of the meeting and say, "Thank you very much for your time" and shake hands before departing. He soon noticed that instead of glowering and grumbling, Jesse-Ray began to thank everyone, too.

Hal pointed out that one never knew what kind of day anyone else was having. No matter how bad your lot, you had no idea how much courage it took for the other person to get out of bed that day. "Their problems may be of a larger magnitude than yours," Hal explained. Jesse-Ray seemed to take the counsel to heart, and Hal noticed how considerately he thanked a salesperson the next time they went to Walmart.

One day, they spent the morning at the community college in Princeton, but events didn't go as expected. They had planned that Jesse-Ray would complete his placements tests, which would solidify his college enrollment for the fall semester. The tests would show the areas in which Jesse-Ray would need remediation. As soon as he took the tests, he'd be placed into remedial classes, which would begin immediately. If he knocked out those remedial classes during the summer, he'd be able to start school at the end of August with the rest of the incoming first-year students.

The sorry news was that Jesse-Ray took the placement tests but scored so low in math, with a grade of twenty-one out of 100, that the guidance counselors couldn't even place him in remediation. He'd be required to bring the grade up to thirty-nine to be eligible for remediation classes. His college career seemed in jeopardy even before it had begun.

Jesse-Ray despaired, believing the score of thirty-nine was an impossible goal, even though it was barely above a failing grade. He had no faith in himself and no interest in rescheduling the test. Hal told him that he could master the material if he applied himself. When I came home that weekend, Jesse-Ray was still fretting about the grade. He was smart, and I wasn't interested in entertaining his whining. Lacking Hal's patience, I told him I would refuse to listen to him continue to predict his own failure.

I suggested he listen to the Schoolhouse Rock songs that could be found on YouTube.

"After seven hours of Multiplication Rock, you'll know your times tables." I said. "You won't even have to study!"

Jesse-Ray dragged his feet, like he dragged his feet about everything.

About the time the low math score appeared to jeopardize his chance to attend college, Jesse-Ray was also alienating his bosses and antagonizing his co-workers at the Bluefield Union Mission. He walked home one Thursday morning, having been told not to come back until Monday. The suspension meant that he would miss three shifts.

For a few hours, he concealed the banishment from Hal. After Hal found out and demanded an explanation, Jesse-Ray professed to be unaware of any behavior on his part to cause the wrath of his supervisors. He was the picture of perplexed innocence.

Hal arranged a meeting with Craig Hammond, the executive director of the Bluefield Union Mission, to discuss Jesse-Ray's situation. The meeting was set for Saturday, so I could attend.

Hal, Jesse-Ray, and I sat down with Craig at a rectangular table in the large open space behind the mission's intake window. This was our first formal meeting. When Jesse-Ray had come into our lives in February, everything had been done on the fly. There didn't seem to be any issues that needed negotiation at the start as Jesse-Ray had expressed a willingness to stay off drugs, and Craig had been on board with our idea to help an aged-out foster child. None of us saw the need to hammer anything out. Now it was early May, and Jesse-Ray's behavior demanded attention.

Workers from the lower-level loading dock and thrift store came and went as we talked. As always at the Bluefield Union Mission, the phone rang incessantly as people called for information or dropped by seeking gas money or food, just as Jesse-Ray had done more than two months earlier.

Craig is a soft-spoken person not given to confrontation. His open-mindedness and quickness to sign on to new ideas explained why he so readily agreed to take Jesse-Ray on as a long-term client. He agreed to this meeting as a checkpoint in the relationship.

As we sat at the table, I recalled that no one knew better than Craig what the opioid crisis had done to devastate Appalachia. Not only did he daily observe clients whose lives had been devastated, but he also had friends and family members who had died of drug overdoses and complications.

At the same time, his experience in running the Bluefield Union Mission, which his late father had operated for decades before Craig took over, helped him recognize and fend off those who seek handouts but do nothing to help themselves.

Hal sat quietly across from Craig. Like Craig, Hal was possessed of a nonconfrontational personality. Sitting around a conference table on a Saturday afternoon was not his idea of a good time, and I knew he wanted a quick end to the meeting along with solid results.

Yet I also knew that Hal would play good cop, because he always played good cop when I was around, even though he grumbled to me about Jesse-Ray's behavior.

The first ten minutes of the meeting were composed of little more than small talk. I wasn't surprised—Craig and Hal might talk tough privately, but their niceness in a group setting was predictable. I hoped they wouldn't leave important things unsaid; it would be kindest to Jesse-Ray to make expectations clear.

Craig offered something mild about not seeing as much progress as he'd hoped for from Jesse-Ray. He touched on complaints from supervisors that Jesse-Ray was failing to carry his weight during his volunteer shifts, that he had been talking too much and was not following directions.

The conversation meandered so I tried to bring it back to the central point.

"This whole arrangement—free food and shelter, intensive mentoring, transportation, and other help—is based on you making strides and improving your prospects," I said to Jesse-Ray.

Craig nodded in agreement.

Several more minutes of conversation ensued, none of which led to outcomes. As the clock ticked, I brought up another matter that required discussion, now that Jesse-Ray had completed his stint in jail but had not yet landed a paying job or successfully enrolled in college.

This meeting occurred before Jesse-Ray and his girlfriend had broken up, and Jesse-Ray had been nagging Hal about wanting to attend his girlfriend's prom. Their late-night conversations were one reason he often overslept.

At my cue, Jesse-Ray repeated the request to Craig, saying that he wanted a ride to the prom because he'd promised his girlfriend. But instead of making an insistent declaration as he had with Hal, his phrasing to Craig was more diffident. The formal setting of the meeting, or perhaps the presence of Craig, cowed him. Hal had become like a parent to Jesse-Ray, someone he could pester.

At first Hal and Craig said nothing, so once again I felt compelled to be direct. I pointed out that for Hal to drive him to Virginia, Hal's costs for gas and wear-and-tear on the Jeep alone would amount to about $100, not to mention the cost of time lost from work for Hal.

"Do you think it's reasonable to expect this from Hal?" I asked Jesse-Ray. I wanted him to consider another person's point of view, to step into Hal's shoes.

He didn't answer.

To his credit, Craig said point blank that the mission would not be providing transportation to the event. Craig also made it clear that if Jesse-Ray decided to take off on his own for the prom, get there by his own devices, and spend the night away from the safe house, he should not plan to come back as a tenant.

"No hard feelings," Craig said. "But if you spend the night away, we'll just assume you've decided to take a different path." I was amazed that Craig laid down the law and glad that the limits he set were firm and clear.

With the prom question settled, I hoped Hal would bring up the touchy topics of Jesse-Ray failing to do laundry and keep the apartment clean. But Hal was content to leave those problems for another day. As disenchanted as Hal was becoming with Jesse-Ray's sloppiness, he wanted to preserve their relationship. He still believed that if they stayed close, he could continue to be a good influence.

Jesse-Ray was subdued. He didn't like what he was hearing, but he didn't object. We all sat in silence for a moment, and I wondered how the meeting would end. I knew that for the aged-out foster-child experiment to have any chance to succeed, we had to be clear about the next steps. So far, Craig hadn't articulated any.

I asked Craig, "What does Jesse-Ray need to do for the Bluefield Union Mission to allow him to stay in the safe house?"

On the spot, Craig created a goal centered on the college-enrollment problem. "Let's see a thirty-nine on the math test by the end of the month," he said.

We walked out of the mission with that objective in mind, something to keep us focused. I was mildly disappointed because of Jesse-Ray's lack of engagement. He hadn't said much during the meeting. I had hoped the conference would be a turning point for him, bringing into focus that we weren't mere bellhops hanging around to carry out his desires. I hoped he'd realize that he was treading in tumultuous waters and that we were the people throwing him a rope. It was his job to grasp it.

The meeting re-energized Hal, though its effect on Jesse-Ray was debatable. As life played out over the coming days, Hal stepped up to the plate to meet the math goal that Craig had set. He bought multiplication flash cards. He quizzed Jesse-Ray daily. Despite Jesse-Ray's doubts, Hal assured him he could master the math.

In solidarity, Hal shared his own childhood experience as a learning-disabled kid with Jesse-Ray. His mother had drilled the times tables into his head during a weeklong cross-country summer trip. It was miserable, but Hal had learned the tables. Half a century later, his memory is undimmed—both of his mother's insistence and the multiplication tables themselves.

On the phone during the week, Hal reported that Jesse-Ray was exhibiting the opposite of the gratitude I'd hoped the meeting would inspire. Instead of viewing the meeting as a reality check, Jesse-Ray had begun muttering about his circumstances, complaining that his life felt like he was on probation. The following weekend, I confronted Jesse-Ray about the grievance.

"This isn't probation," I told him. "This is worse than probation. Probation sets a low bar. When you're on probation, you just have to make sure you don't commit any more crimes. To keep this arrangement going, you have to show active improvement. Emphasis on the active."

For the next couple of weeks, Jesse-Ray settled back into his routine and carried out his shifts at the Bluefield Union Mission. We heard no complaints from supervisors or staff. Hal worried that Jesse-Ray might take off to be with his girlfriend, abandoning everything in Bluefield, but prom night came and went, and Jesse-Ray stayed home without incident.

Then a heartening development occurred on the college front. After mewing and procrastinating and worrying and predicting doom, Jesse-Ray retook the test. He made a ninety-three.

The score was so high it turned out he wouldn't even be required to take a remedial class. The community college would admit him at the start of the semester, in August, based on the strength of his test scores.

Hal showered him with praise. I laughed, learning of the news by phone. Jesse-Ray was smart! I still held a strong belief in his potential.

But as always with Jesse-Ray, the good news was never unalloyed. Because remedial classes weren't required, Jesse-Ray had extra time on his hands—time that he never seemed to use productively. The management team at the Bluefield Union Mission urged him to find an outside part-time job, even something as simple as fast-food service. They wanted him to learn workplace etiquette and other on-the-job attributes. Jesse-Ray never so much as lined up an interview.

As for housekeeping, Hal expected Jesse-Ray to clean up after himself and carry out the simple chores posted on the kitchen wall. Hal set a rise-and-shine time of 8 a.m. every morning, especially Tuesdays, the appointed day to carry the trash bag to the curb and put it in the garbage can. But invariably, Hal would be forced to take care of the trash because Jesse-Ray hadn't gotten up or hadn't bagged up his garbage.

In another incident, Hal let Jesse-Ray use his webcam so that he and his girlfriend could see each other when they talked. He asked Jesse-Ray to turn off the device when he was not using it and put it away so it would not get dirty. Jesse-Ray did neither. He would leave the device on for hours, and the battery would run down. He'd forget to put it away, and then he would pop open his energy-drink cans, spattering sugary liquid on the camera. After a few days, Hal confiscated the webcam.

Hygiene was an issue, too. Hal reminded Jesse-Ray to shower every day, but he'd come out of the apartment in the morning smelling pungent. Staff at the mission complained about his odor, his wild stories, his lack of work ethic, his constant cigarette breaks, and his seeming unwillingness to follow simple directions.

No part of Jesse-Ray's life was up to standard. To improve his poor eating habits, Hal helped him create a monthly food budget to stretch food-stamp money from the first of the month to the thirtieth.

"Get your bread and soda and canned goods free from the mission," Hal told him. "Then spend your money on fresh fruits and vegetables." The advice fell on deaf ears. Jesse-Ray would blow his government food money on pastries, pizza, energy drinks, and white bread sandwiches from the convenience-mart. Hal would make up the deficit when he ran out well before the middle of the month, buying food or cooking for him. I was furious, and we argued over it.

"Am I supposed to let him go hungry?" Hal asked.

"If he goes hungry, then he won't spend all his food-stamp money on junk food in the first two weeks of next month," I said. "If he's inconvenienced, then he'll remember."

But Hal didn't have the heart to let Jesse-Ray go hungry, even temporarily.

Transportation was a continuing burden for Hal as well, even though it was easy and cheap to navigate both Bluefields by bus. But Hal drove Jesse-Ray everywhere he wanted to go. He made shopping convenient by driving him to the grocery store to buy fresh food, even though Jesse-Ray's junk-food diet was impervious to change.

Eventually, Hal began to see that Jesse-Ray was underperforming and began to suspect that things might be falling apart.

At times, Jesse-Ray would act like a sulky teenager. One such night, Hal turned the car around and brought him back to the apartment instead of dropping him off at the Narcotics Anonymous meeting.

"There's no sense in you going if you have an attitude like that," Hal said. "You won't get anything out of it. But you'd better spend the evening getting that apartment shipshape." Hal was annoyed, and Jesse-Ray knew it.

Jesse-Ray would straighten up for a while when he realized he'd pushed Hal too far. The apartment would be halfway presentable for a couple of days, but he'd slack off soon enough.

When the going got tough—especially when he would alienate Hal, the one person always in his corner—Jesse-Ray would fantasize about becoming a drug-numbed drug pusher again. I knew this because Jesse-Ray's poetry would change. In the lines of verse that he emailed me, he would talk about the lure of drugs and drug money. Right before Jesse-Ray went to jail, Hal bought a $35 drug test at Jesse-Ray's request, and Jesse-Ray tested clean. He was thrilled, justifiably proud of his clean-and-sober status. But we lacked the resources to continually monitor him, and as the weeks progressed, we couldn't be sure that he was still clean.

The way he spoke about drugs changed over time as well. After the first month, when I was bemoaning our lack of access to drug testing, Jesse-Ray protested, "You don't understand! I don't want to use drugs!" A few months down the road, his tune changed. "I think that if I lie to myself, it will make things better," he told me. "I think that I don't actually have a problem with addiction. I don't need drugs. I just want them."

Jesse-Ray believed that if he merely "wanted" drugs, then he didn't crave them in the manner of a true addict. Thus, in his mind, he wasn't addicted. Hal and I assumed that drugs were a liability for him, a bad thing. We assumed Jesse-Ray felt the same. But he never spoke of drugs as bad.

He said that when he thought of drugs, he didn't think they were a problem. Rather, drugs were "a solution."

"What problems do drugs solve?" I asked.

"The state of mind that I'm in."

He said point blank, more than once, that even after he finished the drug-free "program" we'd imposed during his time in the safe house, he'd probably smoke weed. And one time he uttered some ridiculous endorsement of hard drugs just to provoke a reaction from me.

When I looked at him in horror, he laughed. "I just said that because you're so anti-drug."

"I'm not anti-drug," I retorted. "I'm pro-Jesse-Ray."

We wondered from time to time whether residential rehab might have turned Jesse-Ray around. We knew that treatment wasn't affordable. And he would refuse to go. But we couldn't help but wonder. Would it have worked?

Hal didn't want to give up on Jesse-Ray. He had seen Jesse-Ray's decent side. One example was when Hal's friend Lawrence Calfee called, urgently needing Hal's help. The police had verified that Lawrence's father had died unexpectedly of natural causes in his Bluefield home, but the body had gone undiscovered for a few days. Heartbroken, Lawrence couldn't bring himself to set foot in the apartment, so Hal was the first of Lawrence's friends to go inside once police and fire department personnel had left. The apartment needed to be cleaned and the furniture cleared out immediately after the body was removed, so the cleaning up was left largely to Hal and another volunteer. Jesse-Ray also refused to enter the apartment, fearing that the sights and smells would bring up memories of his grandmother's death. But he stayed outside with Lawrence, making himself useful and helping to carry the trash and heavy furniture as it was brought outside and carted off.

As Jesse-Ray seemed to flounder—he wrote to me, "I'm trapped in a glass pipe, drowning in the continuing flow of emotion"—Hal and I took stock, wondering if there was more we could do. Since February, when Jesse-Ray had moved in, the Bluefield Union Mission had paid for food and shelter. Hal had provided transportation, a listening ear, and constant moral support. I had been Jesse-Ray's writing and editing coach. Even with that generous package, we knew we fell short of providing the intensive treatment and monitoring that residential rehab would have offered.

Hal did his best to help Jesse-Ray get medical benefits lined up. Jesse-Ray was eligible for mental-health counseling, which we knew he needed because he openly talked with Hal about being depressed. In emails to me, he said that his despairing mind was manufacturing reasons to use drugs again: "I think, 'Just one hit will do!'"

But even after his medical coverage kicked in, no counselor would give him an appointment. Local psychologists and psychiatrists said they didn't have any slots for people on his type of insurance.

So there we were—civilians operating alone in Appalachia, trying to save a depressed and recovering kid from the opioid crisis, grasping and clawing to obtain every government service he was entitled to. And in the end, even when government dollars and insurance coverage came through on paper, the medical profession shrugged. The doctors dusted off their hands.

Was Jesse-Ray doing drugs on the side? We didn't know. Sometimes his hands would shake, which we read on the Internet could be a sign of drug use or sudden withdrawal. Shaky hands could mean a person was using, or it could mean the opposite. Other times his hands were perfectly steady.

What became clear was that he lacked drive, determination, and a desire to apply himself. He faltered even when the steps we asked of him were baby steps.

The emails he sent me continually demonstrated his need for counseling: "I need someone, but I push them away with calm words, pretending I'm okay, when inside I'm screaming, 'Help!'" he wrote. "I deal with everything by self-medication—sedation from all this pain." Hal and I began to feel a sense of helplessness about the situation when it became clear that psychological or psychiatric counseling would not be forthcoming.

Although we tried to shut down his lament about being "on probation," Jesse-Ray took up another line of complaint, which Hal told me on the phone one night. He had groused that Hal and I didn't trust him.

I bristled.

"Just let him say that to me," I told Hal. "If he does, here's what I'm going to tell him. We're not offering trust. We're offering *opportunity*."

I was not only prepared to share that sentiment with Jesse-Ray, but I was also looking forward to it. Jesse-Ray was not going to get the last word, not when I had a retort ready. I felt it was time for another reality check on his road to recovery!

As it turned out, I never got a chance to field Jesse-Ray's complaint about trust. After two back-to-back family visits that took me out of town to see my father in Michigan and my daughter in North Carolina, I headed home to Bluefield. But by then, Jesse-Ray was gone.

Does Medicaid provide counseling to youths in poverty?

Research shows that half of young people in foster care suffer from developmental delays or are in urgent need of counseling. Many aged-out foster children are beset with behavior problems. Many have been exposed to trauma.

Four-fifths of 21-year-olds who suffered child abuse show evidence of at least one mental health disorder.

Behavioral health is one of the foundations of successful transition to adulthood for aged-out foster kids. "If these needs are not met, it is hard to meet other goals like working, going to school, and taking care of family," writes Jennifer Pokempner, child welfare policy director of the Juvenile Law Center.

After completing internships in the US Congress, a group of former foster youths came up with a series of policy recommendations. One of the youths, Yale student Justin Abbasi, urged that two new grants be added to current federal programs.

The first would pay for "trauma-informed, evidence-based psychosocial services." The second would kick in when aged-out foster children accessed those services; it would cover transportation costs and reimbursement for lost wages.

"With more than 20,000 youth aging out of foster care each year, many lose the social supports that underpinned them while in foster care," Abbasi writes. As they transition out of foster care, they must also set up a new support network.

"The federal and state governments have an ethical obligation to ensure that transition-age adolescents who need behavioral health services receive them," he writes.

Even though aged-out foster children such as Jesse-Ray Lewis are technically eligible for behavioral and psychiatric counseling under the Affordable Care Act as well as Medicaid, this "does not guarantee the type of quality, trauma-informed help Abbasi envisions, which is not always present and available to Medicaid recipients," write the editors of The Chronicle of Social Change, which printed Abbasi's proposal. The editors further point out that "Abbasi's proposal is sound in enhancing an existing guarantee, but aging-out youth will need more help than that if mental health is cut out of Medicaid."

Jesse-Ray qualified for health coverage, and the program included psychiatric and psychological services. But despite repeated phone calls to every provider in the Bluefield area in June and July of 2017, no doctor or counselor would give him an appointment. They had no slots for a Medicaid patient, they said.

CHAPTER 14

Eviction day

Stuck in a revolution, spinning
drowning in emotion.
I want to turn the broken dial of my life back
to the same high
most guys hide from
staying up two months straight
hallucinating till my brain is mush.

I'd push my mind to keep going
even if these shadow people kept following me
down an empty street
headlights in the distance.

—Jesse-Ray Lewis, "Mental War"

A heavy-duty black trash bag sat at the curb in front of the safe house. The top story of the two-story house, painted its original pea-green and in need of new coat, was still unfinished inside. The bottom story was now equally empty of human habitation. It was hard to believe it had come to this.

Jesse-Ray had only himself to think about. He not yet reached the age of majority. He had happily traded sleeping under a tree for serviceable indoor accommodations and the chance to live a life of few responsibilities. How could someone who ate most of his meals out of the nearby convenience mart, and who had pledged to clean up after himself, produce so much trash?

The bag's contents provided clues to Jesse-Ray's state of mind. Most of the detritus consisted of food wrappers, leftover junk food, and cigarette butts. The trash bag and its contents were the last traces of Jesse-Ray after Hal spent eight hours cleaning the apartment. Though he was a fast worker, Hal still needed a full day to clean urine off bathroom walls, scrape gum off the hardwood and vinyl floors, and scrub sticky food residue from the once-gleaming expanse of countertop that he had painstaking installed just months before.

Jesse-Ray left other marks in the safe house that felt like punches in the gut to Hal. They were the opposite of a thank-you for his hospitality, hard work, and overeager attempt at what some might call helicopter parenting. Hal had overlooked the first broken window, in the kitchen, which had been cracked during Jesse-Ray's first two weeks in the safe house. Jesse-Ray had said he'd lost his balance and fallen into it and was apologetic over the expense Hal incurred to replace it. "Nothing to worry about," Hal had assured him.

But as Jesse-Ray was preparing to leave, Hal discovered a second smashed window with a baseball-sized hole as if something had been thrown at it. Jesse-Ray had pleaded that it had been an accident, but Hal was convinced that the damage had been caused by carelessness or vandalism.

In the kitchen, where the computer was stationed, the walls and the kitchen's vinyl floor were gouged and pockmarked from Jesse-Ray's careless dragging of the computer chair. The keyboard was gummed up with the sticky remains of food and drink.

The worst insult was a small thing, but it left Hal feeling betrayed because the act was intentional. Hal had installed doorstops to keep the doors from banging against the walls. Jesse-Ray had pried pieces of the spring-steel, flexible doorstops from the walls, unscrewing the metal coils and bending them to fashion a makeshift waterpipe to feed his nicotine habit. This device enabled him to inhale the last traces of burned nicotine from discarded butts. He'd resorted to the practice once he'd run out of money, or things to barter, for cigarettes.

At the same time that he was exhibiting blatant disregard for Hal's property, he was also terminally alienating the staff at the Bluefield Union Mission.

The day Jesse-Ray reached the end of the road with the Bluefield Union Mission, Hal and I were visiting my siblings and my elderly father in Michigan, a visit timed around my father's ninetieth birthday.

Carefree, I was shopping inside a little general store in a picturesque town on Lake Huron during one of our sightseeing days. Hal was tired after our long walk on the pier, where the winds had buffeted us on a surprisingly chilly June day. I'd agreed to duck into the store without him to take a look around while he rested in the car. Visiting small-town general stores with their old-time, homey appearance and vintage products are—to me if not to Hal—part of the fun of traveling. But when I returned to the car, parallel-parked on the main street of the small town, I discovered that Hal had gotten no rest. He was talking on his cell phone, and he wore an expression of consternation. In the twenty minutes I'd been gone, Jesse-Ray's world was building up to a seismic shift.

A few days of our ten-day trip had already passed, with Jesse-Ray content to be on his own and pleased that Hal had given him the minor responsibility of doling out treats to our husky and border collie each day. Hal hadn't trusted him with their food and water; he had assigned that responsibility to a friend.

Jarring Hal's peace of mind on this cold but sunny day, Jesse-Ray had called to say he'd been suspended from work at the mission. This was his second suspension. Hal had smoothed over the first incident in late April by insisting that Jesse-Ray adopt a humble mien, return to the workplace, and apologize to co-workers for showing disrespect. Our meeting at the mission with Craig had occurred on the heels of that first suspension, where we'd hoped to make all expectations crystal-clear to Jesse-Ray. Meredith, Jesse-

Ray's main supervisor, had decided to give him a second chance based on the sincerity of his apology and professed willingness to work harder, and Craig had backed up her decision.

Hal, already done talking with Jesse-Ray when I got in the car, was trying frantically to manage the situation from afar. He was on the phone with Meredith to see if she would reinstate Jesse-Ray again. Hal hated the idea of Jesse-Ray being unsupervised in the safe house while we were gone. We weren't addiction-recovery experts, but we knew that unstructured time for someone in rehab wasn't a good idea.

But Meredith was in an unyielding mood. It seemed that Jesse-Ray's behavior hadn't changed much. His co-workers had repeated their earlier complaints about his sitting around gabbing, goofing off, and failing to be diligent. He completed tasks in a lackadaisical way—if he did them at all. Plus, he would go outside every few minutes to smoke. Further annoying the people around him, his running patter gave the impression he thought himself superior to everyone else in the place.

The conversation ended, and Hal filled me in, telling me that Meredith and the rest of the staff at the Bluefield Union Mission had had it with Jesse-Ray. Hal knew from Meredith's clipped tone and the finality of her words that no matter how much he'd hoped that Jesse-Ray would make progress, nothing at this point would repair Jesse-Ray's relationship with the mission.

Hal, who'd seemed agitated earlier in the call, seemed curiously relieved now that his talk with Meredith had ended.

"You seemed more upset earlier than you are now," I observed. "You weren't able to persuade her to reverse or postpone Jesse-Ray's firing. Why are you so calm? You're acting like everything's okay."

"You don't understand," Hal explained. "They're done with him. It's over. They're never taking him back."

I was too shocked to think of anything to say. I hadn't expected such an abrupt end.

"I'm sure they're going to kick him out of the safe house," Hal continued. "Meredith didn't say they were going to evict him, but I can see it coming. I don't want it to happen while I'm gone. So I told Meredith they needed to let him stay in the safe house until we get back."

Eviction wasn't the focal point of the conversation; work severance was. At the same time, Hal suspected correctly that if Jesse-Ray's work arrangement ended, his free lodging would no longer be tenable as well. Hal wanted to be on hand for Jesse-Ray's move-out day, at least in part to stand guard over his real estate.

Hal, who had repeatedly given Jesse-Ray the benefit of the doubt, had become utterly disenchanted. Jesse-Ray's attitudes hadn't improved and his actions weren't much better. He hadn't read the recommended materials in preparation for college classes; he hadn't sought a part-time paying job, as the mission staff had urged; he hadn't stopped bad-mouthing police, whom he still viewed as the enemy; he hadn't embraced the basic tenet of Narcotics Anonymous to recognize a higher power. This suspension from his shifts at the mission eroded what was left of Hal's trust, and Hal was like a light suddenly switched off—he would no longer play the part of a doting coach or big brother. If the mission was done with Jesse-Ray, so was Hal.

I sat silent, sobered not only because Jesse-Ray was nearing the end of the road, but also by Hal's turnabout, which caught me by surprise.

After posting the three rules in his kitchen for himself, Hal had vowed not to disrupt his own life in a futile attempt to improve Jesse-Ray's. Hal had stopped stepping in to insist that Jesse-Ray make the "right" decisions. He had set more boundaries, such as making it clear to Jesse-Ray that it was up to him to control his own behavior, to work hard, and to conform to the minimal expectations of the Bluefield Union Mission. Step by step, Hal had tried to make his interventions less all-encompassing, passing on more of the responsibility to Jesse-Ray. Hal would remind Jesse-

Ray that he needed to make a doctor's appointment but leave it to Jesse-Ray to make the call. As for showering, Hal would continue to issue reminders, but he would stop short of checking to see whether Jesse-Ray had complied. He would tell Jesse-Ray that wake-up time was 8 a.m., but he would stop banging on the door to rouse Jesse-Ray. He allowed him to oversleep and face the consequences of being late for his shifts at the mission.

Hal had done everything he could to stop being an enabler, and it still wasn't enough.

Though Hal sometimes cut our nighttime talks short because he was exhausted, I was unaware of how burned out he was. Duties and obligations had overwhelmed him, especially as Jesse-Ray himself put out less and less effort. Jesse-Ray had let Hal down so many times that even Hal, a forgiving man, had no charity left. Jesse-Ray's failure was a bitter pill for Hal, who had reasoned and exhorted and stewed over the teenager's problems, striving to maintain a posture of patience and kindness. He'd hoped to see the young man flourish, not flop.

However, Hal was satisfied with the concession from Meredith, who had promised that the mission would refrain from severing Jesse-Ray's living arrangement for a few more days. He agreed with me that it was sad that the Bluefield Union Mission wanted to sever ties with Jesse-Ray, but it had not come as a shock. Hal surmised that they were simply tired of him being lazy and annoying and immature. He felt relieved, knowing that Jesse-Ray would still be in the safe house when we returned after the Fourth of July. Hal would be on hand to help Jesse-Ray cope with news of his eviction and also to supervise his exit.

I hated to worry Hal further, especially as I began to realize the last five months with Jesse-Ray had left him feeling burdened. Brokering the deal with Meredith had actually reduced his stress level. But I couldn't in good conscience let things rest. I was uneasy about the way things were playing out. It was heartening to know that Jesse-Ray wouldn't be thrown out while we were out of town. But what was Jesse-Ray going to do with his freedom from daytime shifts at the Bluefield Union Mission?

"Judging from past behavior, he'll stay up late, eat junk food, hang out with neighborhood kids, and sleep the day away," I said. "That's what he does if you're not there to enforce his routine. And now he's getting a reward for being fired: the gift of free time. He might even bring people into the safe house—drug users."

Hal could see my point. Without Hal to keep him in check, Jesse-Ray would most likely roam around the neighborhood and play basketball, a free-time activity he liked to indulge in whenever he could. He could easily hook up with drug users and dealers, lapsing back into substance abuse. The idea of strangers in the safe house didn't sit well with Hal.

As we sat in the parked car, with a few tourists walking past us in the tiny lakeside town, Hal called Jesse-Ray back and hit the speakerphone button. Together, we suggested that he walk down to the nearby Wade Center, a Bluefield institution devoted to children's activities, to see if they needed volunteers. Jesse-Ray seemed unsure about how to avail himself of this opportunity and conduct a productive conversation with the front office.

"Sell yourself to them as someone who's willing to pitch in and help," I said. "Sell yourself just like you sold those books at the writer's conference."

When we returned to Bluefield, Jesse-Ray said he'd followed our instructions but had been told the Wade Center didn't need volunteers. We never knew if it was the truth.

In the final few days before the Bluefield Union Mission evicted him, Jesse-Ray didn't appear to care about anything. His dirty clothes sat in mounds around the apartment. All Jesse-Ray needed to do was take his clothes to the laundry area at the mission, which was a five-minute walk away, but even that trifling task was too much trouble for him. For months, Hal had issued daily reminders about personal cleanliness and doing his laundry, yet staff members at the mission complained to the end about his questionable hygiene and dirty clothes.

I returned to my job, and Hal took charge of things in Bluefield. He spoke on the phone with Meredith, who confirmed his prediction that Jesse-Ray was no longer welcome in the safe house. Hal didn't intend to question Meredith's authority—or the authority of anyone else at the Bluefield Union Mission—but he wanted to ensure that he wasn't the one delivering the bad news to Jesse-Ray. He asked for another meeting with Craig Hammond because, to Hal, it seemed right that Craig should broker the end of the aged-out foster child project and tell Jesse-Ray exactly why he was being put back on the street.

I missed the final, hastily called meeting at the mission, which occurred on a weekday. Hal filled me in later, starting with the fact that even kind-hearted Craig was forced to agree with his fed-up staff that Jesse-Ray had declined to make the most of the gifts offered.

Craig explained to Jesse-Ray that the end of the road had arrived. Signs of progress that everyone had been waiting to see—a positive attitude, an interest in work—hadn't materialized.

Hal later told me that Jesse-Ray made a halfhearted attempt to speak up for himself. He pointed to the book contract for *Hillbilly Drug Baby: The Poems* as a positive development. Craig agreed that this milestone was something to be celebrated. But he was firm. The Bluefield Union Mission wouldn't continue to underwrite his lodging in the safe house.

In addition to Jesse-Ray's disinterested attitude toward his duties, Hal learned during the meeting that he'd also committed acts of outright insubordination. Once, after Meredith gave him a direct order, he'd wheeled around and showed his back to her. Another time, he'd ignored an assigned task and gone outside to smoke instead. Jesse-Ray's constant excuse was that he'd forgotten what he'd been told.

Even on a slow day, the Bluefield Union Mission was a busy place. It was where people with no other resources turned when they needed clothing, a way to keep their heat from being turned off, an outlay of cash to tide them over during an emergency, or a tank of gas to get to another town. Hundreds of people relied on the food pantry. Enjoying strong community support, the Bluefield Union Mission had been of service to the community's neediest for decades, based largely on the strengths and dedication of its staff and volunteers.

A secondhand store in the rear lower story of the building, facing the alley and abutting the neighborhood, was generally a hopping place, with people picking through the donations and paying a few dollars for kitchen wares, furniture, or used appliances. I once bought a large, like-new George Foreman countertop grill for a couple of dollars, and many similar goods shared rock-bottom prices. Donations came in at a clip. Sometimes goods arrived by the truckload. When things got hectic, all hands needed to be on deck. Often the "all hands" consisted of six or seven people in the loading-dock area, under the watchful eye of a supervisor. The crew might be composed of staff or volunteers or even people assigned by a judge to do community service.

Jesse-Ray failed to prove himself valuable in this milieu. The work assigned to him would not get done. He would mostly sit and talk, and his talk generally consisted of self-aggrandizing topics such as his former drug-dealing days. Or he simply wouldn't be around when he was needed—having gone outside to smoke, again. Even though he impressed his co-workers as canny and smart, he would claim to be confused or say he didn't understand. At the mission, Jesse-Ray wasn't just guilty of braggadocio. According to the staff, he was also disrespectful and insubordinate. He found ways to dodge assignments, take extra breaks, sit around and jaw-bone with the young female staffers, and generally weasel out of tasks.

To make his duties crystal clear, Meredith had written out a list of chores for Jesse-Ray. It included simple tasks such as sweeping up or taking out trash, folding clothes in the thrift-shop section, breaking down cardboard boxes, and helping to unload furniture at the loading dock. The work wasn't complicated. No one needed to be told how to break down the cardboard boxes. They sat on shelves, clearly visible, next to a busy hallway. If they were still in box form, they needed breaking down!

Jesse-Ray was instructed to consult and follow his list, as well as help his crew-mates when a large truckload of donations arrived. But Meredith's list was a good idea that didn't work because Jesse-Ray would check off a task without actually doing it. Or if he did take a stab at something, the execution would be so poor that another staff member would be forced to fix it.

The meeting ended with Craig agreeing to pay for a month at a local motel as a transition step for Jesse-Ray. A driver from the mission would come by the next morning to transport Jesse-Ray to the motel. A new safe house lodger was already lined up to move in the next day, someone who'd lost their possessions in an apartment fire.

Jesse-Ray was glum. I could see it in the photos that Hal took of him after the meeting. After leaving the mission, they'd driven two miles down the road to the abandoned house where Jesse-Ray had first camped out. They needed to take book-jacket photos, which the book publisher had requested. In most of the images, Jesse-Ray appeared solemn, bordering on sullen. Hal coaxed one smiling pose out of him, creating at least one portrait suitable for a publicity headshot.

Now that the situation had played out, the next day couldn't come soon enough for Hal, who knew he would face a hard day's work getting the place back into decent shape.

Just as Jesse-Ray hadn't shown much evidence of assembling a new life during the last five months, he didn't spend five minutes that evening packing his belongings. Instead, he left the organizing to Hal.

Hal entered the safe house on that last morning and began picking up books and clothes. He ignored Jesse-Ray, who sat at the computer desk, crying and trying to engage Hal in conversation. Jesse-Ray seemed to want Hal to rescind the eviction and playing on Hal's sympathies had always worked for him in the past. But not this time.

"I can't do any more for you," Hal said. "It's out of my hands. This place is leased by the Bluefield Union Mission, and it's their decision."

When Jesse-Ray's tears failed to achieve the desired effect, he stopped crying. Hal said nothing, letting it sink in that he wasn't in a position to offer Jesse-Ray another chance.

"I told you I always screw everything up," Jesse-Ray finally said. "Every situation I get in, I fuck it up."

Hal was feeling so disappointed in Jesse-Ray's lack of effort at keeping the place clean that he didn't try to help Jesse-Ray feel better about his plight.

"You can't say you weren't warned. I told you the only person who would get you kicked out of here was you," Hal replied. "Didn't I tell you that every day?" What hurt Hal most was how consistently he'd counseled Jesse-Ray, to no avail.

Jesse-Ray was no doubt startled by Hal's lack of empathy. He'd never witnessed Hal speak with such grim finality, but Jesse-Ray made a final bid for sympathy.

"Am I going to see you again?" he asked. "Are you going to talk to me?"

"At the moment I'm completely disgusted," Hal answered. "I can't believe you disrespected me so much by treating my place this way. You'll have to give me a few days to get over it."

All along, Jesse-Ray had assured Hal that he was sweeping up, throwing garbage away and keeping food wrapped up or refrigerated. Hal had become slightly more vigilant after his first major cleanup intervention, but he still respected Jesse-Ray's privacy and rarely went inside. He would knock on the door at least once a week, but he didn't raise any questions unless he detected a noticeable odor as he approached. If he happened on a mess from time to time, Jesse-Ray would explain it away. He'd say that he'd missed a night of cleaning because he'd been tired and gone to bed early. This lie had been unmasked as Hal scrubbed and scraped away the gummy detritus of Jesse-Ray's filthy living. His excuses about early nights leading to temporary housekeeping lapses had been total fabrications.

From February to the Fourth of July, Hal had listened to Jesse-Ray for hours, driven him all over town (plus the ninety miles each way, to and from jail), arranged for his food stamps and his medical benefits, indulged him, painted a picture of a new life for him, cooked for him, clothed him, taught him hygiene, fussed at him, and counseled him. At the moment of Jesse-Ray's eviction, Hal was forced to embrace the only course of action left: tough love.

Tough love did not come easily to Hal. To mask his own pain at the separation, I believe that he hardened his heart. Just as he had focused on Jesse-Ray's vulnerabilities and charms at the beginning, he now saw with twenty-twenty vision Jesse-Ray's shortcomings, lapses, and manipulations.

When the promised Bluefield Union Mission driver hadn't materialized by late morning, Hal was ready to move things along. He needed to get the apartment in shape for the new lodger, and he couldn't get the job done efficiently with Jesse-Ray underfoot. He wanted to dive into the final phase of the cleaning, and he wanted Jesse-Ray and his accumulated stuff out of the way.

"Come on. Let's go," he said. "Get your things." Jesse-Ray picked up his dingy duffle bag, and Hal grabbed a few items and packed him into the Jeep. They headed to the motel—the same one Jesse-Ray had admitted he'd dealt drugs in for three days—but the room wasn't ready.

While they waited, Hal took care of one last chore for Jesse-Ray. He drove Jesse-Ray to the Social Security office to apply for a new card. Jesse-Ray had lost his card and had put off applying for a new one. Without a Social Security card, not even the minimum-wage employers in town would accept his entry-level applications. And with the Bluefield Union Mission's subsidized lodging about to end, Jesse-Ray's survival would become his own responsibility. He would need that minimum-wage job. With no one paying his rent, Jesse-Ray might finally get serious about supporting himself.

The final chore completed, Hal dropped Jesse-Ray at the motel, helping him carry his things into the small, dingy room. Hal's anger over the trashed apartment had not yet subsided, and he hadn't shed his no-nonsense demeanor. Meanwhile, Jesse-Ray's defenses were back in place, and he wore a mask of indifference, as if he didn't care what was happening.

Their good-bye was brief, concluded with a quick hug and Hal, relenting slightly, saying, "You've got a phone. You can call me any time."

Jesse-Ray just nodded as Hal offered his final words of encouragement. "It's all up to you now. You know what needs to be done to get ready for college next month. You've got a bus pass, and if you go down to the mission, they'll still give you food."

In truth, Hal had mentally and emotionally washed his hands. He'd given more than five months to the Jesse-Ray project. He was done.

Hal and Jesse-Ray's time together had involved much talk, soul searching, negotiating, and boundary setting. Passionate and doting at the beginning, Hal had sacrificed much of his time to become the listening ear and guiding hand he believed Jesse-Ray needed. With equal fervor toward the end, Hal attempted to mend his ways, to stop being an enabler. Hal had availed himself as a coach, a role model, a sounding board, and a teacher. He did his best to withhold judgment and remain encouraging. But something had changed in the last few weeks. As Hal stopped doing things for Jesse-Ray that he could do for himself, he saw that Jesse-Ray was coasting, maybe even stagnating or, even worse, backsliding. Clearly he was not progressing. I'd been pointing this out for a while but Hal had finally started to see for himself.

At some point, Hal had realized that no matter what he did, Jesse-Ray was not going to do his part. I wanted to know when that deflating realization had hit, so when the weekend came, and I came home to a safe house emptied of Jesse-Ray's things, I asked Hal, "When did you give up? What was the turning point?"

I know what the defining moment would have been for me. If I were in Hal's shoes, I would have been livid over Jesse-Ray's failure to line up a ride to the Narcotics Anonymous meetings, even though he knew plenty of people to ask. People at twelve-step meetings are famously collegial, and any one of half a dozen people would have willingly provided transportation. Jesse-Ray had good relationships with the other men who attended, because Hal reported that he smoked and chatted with them after the meetings while Hal sat waiting in the car. One or two of the men had volunteered to become Jesse-Ray's Narcotic Anonymous sponsor, but Jesse-Ray never took them up on the offer.

Delivering Jesse-Ray to the one-hour group sessions, then returning to pick him up, was an extra chore for Hal. After a long day of grueling construction work, he was exhausted and in pain. He wore a hernia belt to try to minimize the discomfort from an earlier surgery, but the fabric support didn't provide much relief. Even so, Jesse-Ray never arranged for his own ride to the meetings, even though Hal asked him repeatedly to do so.

That would have pushed me over the edge. Jesse-Ray's refusal to make transportation arrangements to a meeting a mile down the road was the definitive sign that he wasn't invested in his own recovery. Hal saw it differently. Hal didn't want to be accused of having jeopardized Jesse-Ray's sobriety. He wanted his own conduct to be above reproach. So Hal continued to drive him to meetings.

What was Hal's turning point? It related to the way we had insisted on some spiritual activity each week as part of the rehab program we had cobbled together for the teenager. Jesse-Ray had chosen one-on-one study with Hal over church attendance with me. I'd supported his choice, advising Jesse-Ray that any serious writer could not go wrong by becoming more familiar with the Bible's dramatic stories and poetic images. Plus, Bible study wasn't about trying to convert Jesse-Ray to a religion. The study was aimed to open his eyes to the fact that he wasn't the center of the universe. Hal and I both believed that, unless Jesse-Ray began to rise above the concerns of the material world and to achieve a sense of higher purpose, a negative state of mind would continue to engulf him.

One day, as Hal prepared to begin the weekly lesson, Jesse-Ray told Hal, as if he were doing him a favor, that he could dispense with Bible study. Jesse-Ray had decided that he wasn't into it. The instruction was a waste of his time and Hal's.

"I shut the Bible, gathered up my books and study materials, and told him to have a nice rest of his day," Hal recalled.

For Hal, Jesse-Ray's declaration was the final indicator of apathy. As Hal put it, "It became clear to me right then that he did not give a shit about anything."

Appalachians: Many may buckle under the weight of stereotypes

No other recent publication has rivaled J.D. Vance's bestselling book, the 2016 memoir *Hillbilly Elegy*, in sparking polarizing reviews because Vance's approach inflames passions about Appalachian stereotypes. Vance signals his willingness to ignite debate in the book's title, employing the word "hillbilly." Though the connotation is changing, it has long been employed by outsiders as a slur to ridicule mountain folk. A New Republic writer says the book is "little more than a list of myths about welfare queens repackaged as a primer on the white working class. Vance's central argument is that hillbillies themselves are to blame for their troubles."

Ironically, Vance may have inspired changes to the language itself, as the "hillbilly" epithet is newly showing up in favorable contexts, demonstrating the lightning speed at which the English language can shapeshift. For instance, "hillbilly" appears in a major international newspaper's story about former coalminers who are learning the skill of computer coding, a trend that has led to the nicknaming of a Kentucky region as "Silicon Holler." In the story, a 55-year-old coder who spent thirty years in the coal mines says, "A hillbilly is someone who is hard-working, thoughtful, and loyal. And rugged. Because we've seen some tough times."

In interviews, Vance related that the first instinct of many people in the region is often to discard their hillbilly-ness out of shame; after the publication of his book, many of his family members have decided to newly embrace their roots.

This new, positive spin is the opposite of what "hillbilly" telegraphed in times past. Not only does the term conjure up a person who lacks sophistication, but it also plants them squarely in a particular region: the backwoods. Abject poverty is always part of the stereotype. The cartoonish Li'l Abner and Snuffy Smith characters may be the butt of jokes, but the 1972 movie "Deliverance" was no laughing matter. For almost half a century, its portrayal of mountain folk as uneducated, backward, and deviant has remained seared in the American consciousness.

Works like *Hillbilly Elegy* keep stereotypes alive. Vance, a Yale Law School graduate who grew up poor in Appalachia, sows discord with his views about poverty and addiction and whether society should step in to solve Appalachia's problems; some blame the government and lack of economic opportunity, while Vance implies that character flaws and bad choices doom individuals to dead-end lives. Covering similar territory, the 2017 movie "The Glass Castle," featuring movie stars Brie Larson and Woody Harrelson, depicts the true story of a drug-wrecked family who lived in squalor for a time in West Virginia, squatting in hovels similar to those in Jesse-Ray's community of origin.

Appalachian accents also generate stigma. Krislin Nuzum, a member of the West Virginia Dialect Project, says that outsiders underestimate and undervalue Appalachians because of the way they speak, which takes "a toll on a person's self-confidence and their self-worth."

According to Kirk Hazen, a linguistics professor at West Virginia University, "In the US there are two dialects that are overwhelmingly seen as negative—Black English and southern English. They're seen as negative because the speakers themselves are seen negatively in US society."

A 2014 National Public Radio story argues that "movement toward a more holistic regional picture may be a strong step toward tackling the larger societal ills." That prospect may have seemed imminent in 2014—less so now. Starting in November 2016 and continuing today, national and international news media have documented a red-state voting bloc, more rural and less educated than other segments of the electorate, which provided the electoral base for US President Donald Trump, who declined to distance himself from white nationalist and even white supremacist groups, even after taking office. Photos of Trump supporters carrying racist and misogynist signs only cemented the image of Appalachians as lower class, white, and undereducated.

Did the force of history, demographics, and popular culture create a crushing weight on Jesse-Ray Lewis? Stereotypes might be described as a cruel joke, but can they also act as a yoke?

For all his professed desires to keep a roof over his head and his justifiable pride at moments when Hal praised him for his achievements, Jesse-Ray nevertheless found himself enmeshed in the trap of society's low expectations.

CHAPTER 15

The way ahead

People with no needle tracks say they know
what rock bottom is.
Do they know what it's like to sleep abandoned
by everyone
but surrounded by everyone?

I slept in a house whose foundation was vile
on a ground made of maggots and the spit of the
vengeful.

They spit on the grave of a lost boy.
—Jesse-Ray Lewis, "Utterances from the Present"

The black plastic bag filled with Jesse-Ray's trash, which the city had picked up on garbage day, was long gone by the time I arrived home for the weekend. But on the back porch sat enough material for an anthropological excavation: a second fifty-five-gallon bag full of towels and clothes, which I insisted that Hal open.

"Smells like cat piss," he grumbled. Untying the knot, Hal took a step backward.

"How could it smell like cat piss?"

"I don't know. Maybe he let a cat in to piss on his things." Hal's mood hadn't yet improved since Jesse-Ray's ouster. He was sad but pretending to be impassive and stolid. I knew this because Hal is normally a warm, touchy-feely person. It was unlike him to answer my questions in such a clipped way. He showed little appreciation for my almost obsessive desire for a postmortem as I sought clues to Jesse-Ray's psyche, even clues that a bag of dirty laundry might harbor.

I held my breath as I poked around in the bag, wanting to confirm Hal's observation that Jesse-Ray had left behind good stuff, including clothes. It was true. He'd abandoned bath towels and designer shirts I'd bought him from thrift stores as well as Hal's purchases of new blue jeans, socks, and underwear—useful items, all. Jesse-Ray had acquired a serviceable wardrobe during his time with us, some of it from clothing he'd picked out at the mission and some that we'd bought. In the end, he didn't value it enough to run it through the mission's washing machine and take it with him.

After probing through the plastic bag, I still had questions. I wasn't completely sorry to see Jesse-Ray go. Jesse-Ray's needs and wants had impacted our life as a couple and monopolized our conversations. The emotional wear and tear on Hal had been hard to witness. Because he'd been in the trenches with Jesse-Ray, Hal had taken it personally when the Bluefield Union Mission cut ties with him. But Jesse-Ray had taken Hal for granted, at best, and taken advantage of him, at worst, and I was happy to see Hal relieved of that trial. I was sorry that Hal had lavished affection and attention and a little money on Jesse-Ray only to face defeat.

I wasn't as devastated as Hal was by Jesse-Ray's departure because I believed my email relationship with Jesse-Ray would probably survive the physical split. And yet I was frustrated not to have a chance for a final interview with Jesse-Ray. I wanted to hear from his lips why he'd engineered things in such a way to make his eviction inevitable. More than anything, I was baffled at Jesse-Ray's departure. No matter from what angle I viewed the situation, Jesse-Ray's lack of willingness to seize opportunity and work to improve his circumstances made no sense to me. He hadn't met the relatively low bar everyone had set for him. I couldn't fathom Jesse-Ray's passing up the golden ticket the Bluefield Union Mission had handed him with the grant of free food and lodging. It was equally distressing to later learn that, in addition to other services that he'd lined up with Hal's help, Jesse-Ray had walked out on a community college education that would have been paid for by the federal government.

Didn't the fact that he'd cried the morning of his leaving mean that he didn't want to go? Or were the tears an attempt to manipulate? Was Hal a mark to him, right up to the end?

I especially couldn't reconcile the idea that Jesse-Ray had forsworn his writing talent. His manuscript for *Hillbilly Drug Baby: The Poems* was completed. The contract was signed, the verses professionally edited, the publisher happy. More than a half-dozen potential book cover designs using Hal's photographs had been presented to Jesse-Ray for inspection and approval. Hal and I had tried to convey our sense of excitement, but Jesse-Ray failed to display much interest. At Hal's urging, just days before he was booted from the safe house, Jesse-Ray sent a terse but courteous reply to the publisher telling her to choose the version she liked for the cover. We don't know if Jesse-Ray even opened the book-cover designs on his computer, though the subject matter should have been compelling—most of the designs prominently featured photos of him.

In the first few months, Hal wasn't always receptive to my opinions about Jesse-Ray, usually offered at night over the phone, sixty miles away, when everyone was tired from the day. My advice ran along the lines of Hal's needing to hold Jesse-Ray accountable to wake-up times and cleanup rules. Plus, I objected to Jesse-Ray's lack of respect for Hal and appreciation of his efforts. A foundation of twelve-step efforts is the "attitude of gratitude," an outlook on life that encourages thankfulness and eschews blame. Those who fail to adopt it risk sabotaging their recovery.

My mostly unsolicited advice evoked a predictable reaction in

Hal—he changed the subject. "I've been dealing with him all day. I don't walk to talk about him now," he'd say. Hal didn't always want to discuss Jesse-Ray with me, partly because I was predictably critical of his approach.

"He's depressed," Hal would say. "He never got any good teaching or role modeling at home." Or, "He needs counseling. He's still recovering from drugs. His brain's not right yet."

Hal was taken aback when I commented once that, "You're nicer and more patient with Jesse-Ray than you are with me!" That observation held enough truth to give Hal—who devotes effort to being a considerate husband—pause.

After he fell behind on his construction projects and saw little reciprocal effort from Jesse-Ray, Hal was more open to changing his stance. He began to understand the perils of enabling a recovering addict. But once Jesse-Ray was out of the safe house, Hal was not inclined to give him one more moment of time or to make any further emotional investment in the situation.

Hal's postmortem was black and white. "He saw how much work it would take to change," Hal told me. "He wasn't interested." For Hal, that was the end of the story. While I was intent on finding answers to why and how Jesse-Ray had stumbled so badly, Hal didn't want to talk about the questions.

As a result, Hal's reaction came as no surprise when, the day after the eviction, Jesse-Ray called to ask if Hal would drive to the motel to bring him a gold chain he'd left behind.

Hal said no. He'd take it down to the mission, and Jesse-Ray could pick it up from there.

"The mission gave you a bus pass," Hal said. "Use it. You can ride all over Bluefield and even to Princeton for free." I had been urging Hal for months to make that statement instead of acting as Jesse-Ray's chauffeur, and finally he had.

At first, Jesse-Ray tried to push past Hal's brusqueness. During the first week after his eviction, he called Hal at least once a day to ask for rides or bemoan the fact that he'd run short of cigarettes. Hal hung tough. Hal's Jeep was no longer the Jesse-Ray-mobile. He told Jesse-Ray he must figure things out for himself. He would turn the questions around, asking, "Do you have a plan for what you'll do when your thirty days at the motel are up?" Jesse-Ray did not.

Once or twice, Hal spotted him in the neighborhood near our house, hanging out with some of the high-school kids, a year or two younger than himself. It appeared that Jesse-Ray wasn't doing anything to be productive. In fact, even though his only responsibility was to safeguard his food-stamp card, he promptly lost it. When his new one came in the mail, Hal took it down to the mission for Jesse-Ray to retrieve.

With more time on his hands and a weight off his shoulders, Hal threw himself back into renovating the upper story of the safe house, hammering and running electrical wires and repairing radiators and performing other tasks he'd neglected. As Hal settled back into his routine, the next place I went for answers was to the Bluefield Union Mission. I dropped by on a Saturday afternoon hoping to meet with Craig, the executive director, and Meredith, the person who'd most closely supervised Jesse-Ray.

Speaking with them separately, I found a curious unity in their views.

I asked them the same set of questions: Did they have any regrets? Did they think Jesse-Ray had bamboozled us? Should we have seen at the beginning that the case would not end well?

"We felt sorry for him when we first met him," Meredith said. A diminutive woman with a ready smile, she was the supervisor of a crew of tough workers—some longhaired, some tattooed, most of them street smart—on the lower level of the mission that encompasses the thrift shop and loading dock. She recalled the cold day when Jesse-Ray walked in off the streets, flushed, under the weather, and hungry. He told them about his status as an aged-out foster child. The staff wanted to help him.

But months of failing to perform his duties had eroded the goodwill of his co-workers. Irritated, they made a steady pilgrimage up the stairs to complain to Meredith. "They'd say that he was not working and that we needed to get rid of him," she reported. "I would go downstairs and show him what to do. As long as I was with him, he'd do his work. But the minute I left, he stopped."

In the thrift-store area—a cavernous room with a cement floor, shelves against the wall, bins of clothing in the middle, and furniture stacked all around—he'd make himself comfy near the check-out desk.

"He would sit with the girls instead of doing what he was supposed to do," Meredith said. "He would go outdoors to smoke all the time."

Co-workers also complained that his hygiene was lacking, even though he had access to free shampoo and soap from the mission. "All he had to do was ask," she said.

"He had to do only three things to keep the arrangement going, right?" I asked. "Keep himself clean, keep the safe house clean, and not be a total jerk when he came here for his shift."

"That's right," Meredith confirmed.

How much easier could life be? Could a bar be set lower? I was still puzzled. Both times Jesse-Ray had been suspended from his volunteer shifts, he'd professed bewilderment to Hal over what he'd done wrong. But even a child could understand the minimal expectations that were in force.

Asked if we had let the situation carry on too long, Meredith said, "We gave him the benefit of the doubt. We did the best we could to help him. He wasn't willing to accept a new way of doing things."

But she didn't regret giving Jesse-Ray a second chance, and neither did Craig.

"I think it's good that we did what we did over five-and-a-half months," Craig pronounced. "I'm glad we tried as long as we did. He's a twisted, tortured soul, but he also was playing us." Craig stopped for a moment. His eyes gleamed as he broke into a smile. "*That*, in a way, I have to give him points for. That's a skill set."

Hal and I both knew what Craig meant by "playing us." Jesse-Ray had a penchant for postponing judgment day. A master of the plausible excuse, he was adept at dodging blame. He was always saying that he was confused or didn't understand or—perhaps the most frequent justification—he forgot. Over time it became clear that Jesse-Ray was actually rarely confused. And he never forgot things that were important to him—like the fact that he could get a nickel off cigarettes at the Joy Store. He also never forgot what time he was supposed to meet his buddies in the neighborhood to play basketball.

In the end, Craig and Meredith agreed on an assessment. "He stayed here as long as he could while doing as little as possible," Meredith said. "He acted like he was here because he had to be here, not because he wanted to be."

The month after he was evicted from the safe house, Jesse-Ray spent much of his time floating around Bluefield, dependent on acquaintances. "We see him," Meredith said. "Sometimes he stops by to get food. His girlfriend drives him."

The existence of a girlfriend was news to me and Hal. Apparently, he'd taken up with a woman sometime during his final days at the mission.

The college semester was set to start in late August. In a phone call to Hal, a week or two after his ejection, Jesse-Ray told Hal that he planned to attend. I wondered if there was a shred of hope that Jesse-Ray would keep his word. If he did start college, grant money would pour in from the government, and renting a room or apartment would be possible. Yet, with a half-dozen people helping him, he hadn't carried out simpler tasks. Without mentors, wranglers, and guardians, how would he get himself to class on time, alert, groomed, and ready to learn?

The end of August came and went. Despite his telling Hal that he planned to show up for class, he didn't. We found out later that he wasn't even in town when the semester started. Apparently, he'd made the college declaration because he'd thought Hal wanted to hear it.

After talking with Meredith and Craig, I felt reassured that everyone believed we'd done the right thing in staying the course for as long as possible. But their insights didn't give me the answers I was looking for. We had started with so much hope—where had it gone? A clear path to upward mobility had seemed within Jesse-Ray's grasp. I wanted to talk with him one more time. I wanted to ask, "Why did you let it all go?"

In their final phone call, Hal invited Jesse-Ray to call him again, if he liked, to set up a time to meet and talk in person. But Jesse-Ray never followed through. When Jesse-Ray fell completely out of range, we would have no way of contacting him. Then we found out that the motel owner had thrown him out for trashing the room before the thirty days was up.

Jesse-Ray had been at the motel for less than three weeks when he'd sunk into his customary state of squalor. Livid, the motel owner called the mission seeking the green light to evict Jesse-Ray, and they had granted it, understanding that history had repeated itself. The motel room stank from cigarette butts littered everywhere, even on the bed, and from food strewn all over the place. Hal and I heard that it had taken several hours of cleaning before the room could be inhabited again.

Jesse-Ray showed up on foot at the mission, appealing again for help, employing the same excuses he'd used on Hal: He'd failed to clean up his mess from the night before because he'd been tired and gone to bed early. It was just one night's mess, he maintained.

The excuse didn't fly. Jesse-Ray was out on the street again.

Then, sometime in August, he stopped by Bluefield Union Mission to pick up a check from the government—a $200 income-tax refund from a fast-food job he held in 2016. A couple of months earlier, Hal had helped him acquire his W-2s and fill out the paperwork to claim the refund.

I was forced to come to terms with the fact that no one could answer the question of "Why?" No one could explain why things had turned out this way or why Jesse-Ray had behaved as he had. But one chilling memory kept returning. As I pondered it, I realized that Jesse-Ray himself might have given me the answer not long after he was released from his stint behind bars.

It was something he'd said, something I'd discounted at the time. While in the lockup, he was frantic. He'd called for Hal to pick him up and, when his phone privileges ran out, he'd convinced other inmates to give him their phone time and make a call to us. "He's scared," an inmate told us on Jesse-Ray's behalf. "You need to come get him."

Jesse-Ray had acted as though he couldn't stand five minutes behind bars, much less tolerate a sentence befitting his crimes. When I spoke to him afterward about the experience, I seized on his antipathy toward jail to bring up the concept of hitting bottom, which some professionals in the recovery field believe is necessary to motivate an addict to tackle the tedious tasks of establishing an ordinary life.

Jesse-Ray was smoking a cigarette in the front yard when I suggested that the prospect of a return to jail might motivate him to clean up his act. After all, if he reverted to his previous lifestyle, he could look forward to the typical length of a drug-crime sentence, which was three years, according to the Bureau of Justice Statistics.

"Maybe with this, you've hit bottom," I suggested, brimming with optimism. "You hate jail so much that you're now willing to make changes."

He gave me the sidelong glance that meant a pronouncement was coming.

With certainty and vehemence, he said, "I'm a long way from hitting bottom."

The new controversy about "hitting bottom"

A bedrock belief of the recovery program Alcoholics Anonymous is that addicts and alcoholics must "hit bottom" before they're truly willing to seek treatment.

In AA literature, the assumption that "few people will sincerely try to practice the AA program unless they have hit bottom" is a given. Why? The literature strings together a series of questions that paint an honest picture of the alcoholic or addict in the throes of the disease:

"Who wishes to be rigorously honest and tolerant? Who wants to confess his faults to another and make restitution for harm done? Who cares anything for a Higher Power, let alone meditation and prayer? Who wants to sacrifice time and energy in trying to carry AA's message to the next sufferer? No, the average alcoholic, self-centered in the extreme, doesn't care for this prospect—unless he has to do these things in order to stay alive himself."

Many treatment providers agree about advising family members not to swoop in to protect the alcoholic from negative consequences, because in doing so they hasten their loved one down a destructive spiral that may end in death.

However, a new trend challenging the concept of standing back while a loved one hits bottom stems from the fact that hitting bottom, for some, can be fatal. Each addict's perception of bottom is unique to him or her.

Addictions expert and author Debra Jay has witnessed a number of people hitting bottom, including a college-educated, divorced father who lost everything and repaired to his parents' basement to drink and smoke pot each day; a young man who traded his girlfriend's new car for crack cocaine; a young father who went to bed drunk and suffocated on his own vomit; a 72-year-old grandmother who went outside half naked and passed out; and a mom who drove drunk with her babies in the back seat to buy more wine. (In the latter case, the police stopped her and took the babies into protective services and the mom to jail.)

Jay argues that hitting bottom should never be the first tactic. "Only when every reasonable intervention technique is exhausted should we let someone freefall. Even then, there are ways to raise the bottom, to stretch out the safety net of treatment and recovery," she says. She calls it "a strategy of last resorts."

Others are more militant in trying to repudiate the concept of hitting bottom, questioning the assumption that addicts and alcoholics must reach a dangerously high level of desperation before treatment will work. In New York Magazine, Jesse Singal writes, "It's clear that few misconceptions about addiction have led to as much unnecessary trauma and harm as this one."

Maia Szalavitz, author of the book *Unbroken Brain*, argues that addiction isn't a moral failing or a disease but rather a learning disorder, as addicts and alcoholics learn that drugs or alcohol help them cope or make them feel good.

When we asked Jesse-Ray how he endured the traumas of his childhood, he confessed that, awash in a haze of drug-induced euphoria, he barely noticed what was happening around him, much less thought to question it. Drugs anesthetized him, enabling him to stay perpetually numb.

Debra Jay points out that, "The addicted brain can't make lasting connections between alcohol and the problems it causes. Once the problems go away, alcohol is their best friend again. Addiction is both invisible and sacred to alcoholics: they deny its existence yet sacrifice everything to it."

As for hitting bottom, "350 people a day find a bottom with no bounce: death," writes Jay. "Countless others go to prison, go insane, or just go nowhere."

If addiction experts are split, friends and family members may turn to the federal government for answers. But the US government's judgment about intervention is bleak. "There is no evidence that confrontational 'interventions' like those familiar from TV programs are effective at convincing people they have a problem or motivating them to change. It is even possible for such confrontational encounters to escalate into violence or backfire in other ways."

A government website advises that, "Instead, you should focus on creating incentives to at least get the person to a doctor. Often people will listen to professionals rather than have conversations with friends and family members, as the latter encounters can sometimes be driven by fear, accusations, and emotions."

If we don't allow the addict to hit bottom, what is the alternative? Some addiction experts maintain that family, friends, or employers can effectively compel an addict to embrace treatment, offering crumbs of hope to suffering families. A Hazelden Foundation study asked sober alcoholics what had inspired their recovery; more than three-quarters said a friend or relative had intervened.

CHAPTER 16

How we are changed

I had a career as a dealer.
Now I'm the fiend
trying to get the hit.
—Jesse-Ray Lewis, "Depression"

Had we become jaded after devoting almost half a year to Jesse-Ray? I wasn't sure. I didn't want to believe that Jesse-Ray had been a manipulator and we his puppets.

One of the younger workers at the Bluefield Union Mission doubted Jesse-Ray's motives from the start. "We just gave him a five-month vacation from his previous life" was his cynical but clear-sighted assessment.

If that was true, then Jesse-Ray harbored no other motive than to squeeze whatever material goods and services he could from the willing adults who surrounded him at the Bluefield Union Mission and the safe house. I didn't want to accept that scenario. Jesse-Ray had seemed sincere, bordering on grateful—at least at the beginning. He had seemed open to change.

Had it been a mirage?

I saw a change in Hal after Jesse-Ray's departure. He grew more skeptical, in sharp contrast with his earlier willingness to believe almost anything Jesse-Ray said. Hal had listened attentively to Jesse-Ray's wretched descriptions of child abuse along with the more farfetched tales of drug lords, gangs, and riches.

When Hal shared with me the story of the buried gun, and when

Jesse-Ray first described the drug kingpin named Rick, I cautioned Hal not to take Jesse-Ray's word for anything without trying to verify the facts. Regardless, Hal got caught up in the stories of Jesse-Ray's drug-riddled childhood, violent father, and teenage apprenticeship in a meth gang. When I came home one weekend, Hal told me the story of Jesse-Ray's supposed ownership of a Mercedes-Benz with $300,000 stashed inside—a car with a secret compartment that concealed contraband and cash. Jesse-Ray had told Hal he was planning to call a friend in Colorado to have the car delivered to him. The tale was so unbelievable that I laughed outright. And yet Hal was halfway tempted to believe the story. Only after a few weeks passed without Jesse-Ray's car showing up did Hal come to realize it was a lie.

At first Hal also believed Jesse-Ray's declaration that his buried gun still lay in the earth near the abandoned house. Hal, having fired guns for sport and recreation throughout his life, eventually noticed Jesse-Ray's utter lack of familiarity with firearms. Halfway into Jesse-Ray's stay, Hal concluded that the gun probably never existed.

"I just got to where I didn't believe anything he said," Hal said when I asked him about how he had felt during Jesse-Ray's final days in the safe house.

Hal also became convinced of the efficacy of tough love, even if the realization came too late to influence his work with Jesse-Ray. At first, Hal thought he was helping Jesse-Ray by attending to his needs. Sometimes Jesse-Ray confessed that he was troubled that Hal did so much for him; once he even said that he wanted to pay Hal back. But even when Hal became visibly weary from helping him from the morning to the evening, Jesse-Ray did nothing to relieve him by accepting more responsibility himself.

By the time we left for our Michigan trip in late June, Hal was close to the breaking point. He had allowed himself to be sucked into demands that were all-enveloping. It was finally dawning on him that Jesse-Ray wasn't doing his share. But Hal resolved that he'd hang in there as long as the Bluefield Union Mission was on board.

Watching Hal agonize over his role was like an arrow in my heart. Hal had pinned many hopes on Jesse-Ray, most likely because he himself would have prized a kindly adult coming to his aid when he was a disoriented seventeen-year-old in Miami almost five decades ago. In Jesse-Ray, Hal had created a stand-in for his younger self; someone he could guide and lavish affection upon, enjoying the pleasure of watching a young life redeemed.

Sometime during the final two months, I asked Jesse-Ray, "You know how Hal would react if you got kicked out of here or started using drugs again, don't you?" I knew the answer would shake him, given his view of Hal—who could build things, rig things up, cut down trees, and operate heavy equipment—as a tough guy.

"He'd be mad," Jesse-Ray said.

"He would *cry*," I said. "He'd cry *tears*."

Jesse-Ray blinked. This was not the answer he'd expected.

Gradually, Hal began to extricate himself from his entanglements by adhering to the three guidelines he'd posted in our kitchen, even though holding back didn't come naturally to him. He began to understand the limits of our amateur intervention as the depths of Jesse-Ray's traumas and twisted thinking became clear, especially his inability to envision a productive future.

Rereading Jesse-Ray's writings, I came across chilling lines that coincided with Hal's assessment that our continued intervention would achieve nothing because Jesse-Ray's problems were too deep: "It's a race to the finish line, crying violent thoughts of repressed memories so fucked up it would take a team of therapists and three straitjackets to make them understandable to an undamaged brain." And in the poem "Pain," he wrote, "Five million life tests and I've failed all of them."

Witnessing Hal's hurt at Jesse-Ray's lack of follow-through was tough for me, but at the same time, I was glad that Hal had had an opportunity for emotional growth. The hardest thing for Hal was to learn the detrimental nature of enabling. It hurt him to realize that when he went the extra mile for Jesse-Ray, the effect was often harmful.

I couldn't resist asking Hal if he had ruled out ever helping an aged-out foster child again. After what we'd been through with Jesse-Ray, I thought he might be angry with me for even suggesting it. I was surprised to hear an answer showing he'd already thought about the possibility. He'd even set conditions that he would place on any young recovering addict who might end up in the safe house, should we ever be tempted to open up our lives again.

"What would those conditions be?" I asked.

"If there is ever a next time, they're going to have to show me," Hal said. "Next time, I'm not driving them down to their [Narcotics Anonymous] meetings—they can walk or take the bus. If they want it, they're going to have to go after it. It's up to them to do the work, not me."

On one topic, Hal took the opposite stance from Meredith's and Craig's. In contrast to the leaders of the Bluefield Union Mission, Hal wasn't okay with the fact that Jesse-Ray had strung us along for months. Hal now sided with Jesse-Ray's coworkers, who'd long lobbied for him to be given the boot.

"Do you think that checks, balances, and consequences might have unmasked Jesse-Ray as someone who was never going to step up, had they been introduced earlier?" I asked him.

"Absolutely," Hal answered without hesitation. "If we had to do it all over again, he wouldn't have lasted two weeks."

As for me, I would have done things differently as well. I would have paid attention to clues. As I picked through emails, poems, and interview notes as part of my postmortem, I saw patterns. Jesse-Ray's true state of mind emerged in his words, and his outlook pointedly lacked references to will, work, or change. In fact, the more I perused, the more I saw that he pined for his prior life.

He spoke of his drug-dealing days with relish and bravado. He boasted about his survival skills. He said that he knew how to protect himself. He described how he avoided being jumped or arrested while running drugs. "I might do illegal shit all day, but once I get a sketchy vibe, I'm out." He was proud of his street smarts.

He also unapologetically called himself a "couch hopper"—someone who was clever when it came to ingratiating himself into people's lives. "If you told me to find someplace else to stay, I guarantee you I could find two different houses within three days," he once boasted.

Those lines came as a jolt. Jesse-Ray was all but defining himself as a con man, skilled and willing to inveigle others to come to his aid. Perhaps this was the hustler side of Jesse-Ray that Hal and I had been blind to but my friend Saundra Kelley had recognized.

I found equally telling material in an email Jesse-Ray had sent me, where he'd voiced what now looked to me like an escape fantasy. "I've got a place where I'm safe, but I want to get out and see the world," he wrote. A similar sentiment popped up in a poem where he mentioned his yearning to live "in the woods again." I'd glossed over it at the time, but now it was plain: Even as he professed to appreciate the roof over his head, Jesse-Ray longed to be elsewhere. He was never 100 percent committed, never all-in with the program.

I had looked past those phrases, choosing instead to focus on his statements that signaled progress. I believed I was witnessing transformation. For instance, he'd said that even if people called him a crack baby, "that's not who I am." I had fooled myself into believing that he had come to see the downside of substance abuse when he wrote in an email that "even drugs never made lonely thoughts disappear."

Just days before the Bluefield Union Mission kicked him out of the safe house, Jesse-Ray sent me an email where he described his yearning for people-filled rooms rather than "emptiness and dust." He seemed to be counting his blessings, including the value of "a place that is run on the love of hearts that I never knew existed." On some level, Jesse-Ray knew that Hal and I cared for him.

Knowing he experienced such moments, I was sad for the "lost boy" of his poems. "I want to be the kid I never got to be. I want to see things in a soft light," he once wrote. "I'm honestly afraid of what my future holds. I hope whatever it is I can live in it and not want to die every minute."

His writing, conversation, and behavior clearly showed that Jesse-Ray's vision wasn't synchronous with ours. We'd imagined Jesse-Ray with a community college degree, a solid job, a drug-free life, and a future that, if it were to include family, would find Jesse-Ray capable of being a decent father. Maybe our vision wasn't right, but we felt we were on the side of the angels. Who's to say? We couldn't restore his childhood. But we had tried to demonstrate the worth of hard work and model a sense of wonder at the world.

Sadly, Jesse-Ray never took the first step that must precede all other steps. He never agreed to do the work.

Yet who can blame us for hoping that he might acknowledge his own brilliance, work to develop his prodigious talent, and reject the life of a drifter and a grifter? I still miss his lopsided grin and his quick retorts. Who can blame us for believing a miracle might happen?

Is the Story Ever Over?

As Hal and I cast about for the meaning of Jesse-Ray's journey to the Bluefield Union Mission and our safe house, we kept coming back to inevitable realities. Success was impossible as long as Jesse-Ray declined to meet minimal expectations and do his part to piece together a new life for himself.

For a few months, that life seemed within reach—at least from our point of view. That life involved breaking the hold of illegal drugs, embracing higher education, and being able to pay his bills via legal employment.

But was it fair to lay blame at Jesse-Ray's doorstep, to hold him accountable for failing to do the requisite work? Was it his fault he ignored his talents and turned his back on those who offered help?

Professionals who work with first-generation college students who are substance abusers or who come from violent backgrounds often encounter troubled psyches like Jesse-Ray's. Fran Bennett Clark, who directed the Upward Bound program at West Virginia University before moving to a similar job in 2017 at Virginia Tech, offers piercing insights based on more than a decade's worth of experience dealing with troubled youth and those who may be the first in their families to head to college.

Speaking hypothetically, she paints an alternate reality in which Jesse-Ray's reactions seemed predictable, even if not rational to others. "His normal was that everybody in his life was on drugs," she says.

While she did not meet Jesse-Ray, her professional expertise involving first-hand contact with addicts makes her believe that when young people are on the brink of a more rewarding life, some move forward; others don't.

She also offers three additional insights from her work with troubled youth:

First, "Often with people who have been through so much in their lives, they are as much addicted to the chaos as the drugs. If your body gets attuned to having that adrenaline, it feels bizarre, and it can be weirdly uncomfortable when life becomes calm, and you're not having to deal with one difficulty after another," she says.

Second, squalor and poor hygiene could be symptoms of an underlying depression or other mental disorders. "For someone who's depressed, it can be overwhelming even to brush your teeth," she says. For people who have struggled with mental health problems for virtually their entire lives, a sort of paralysis can set in—which may appear to outsiders as laziness and a lack of commitment.

Third, a person may be stuck in a situation that appears to others as dysfunctional, abnormal or even dangerous, yet his or her commitment to change may be lacking. "You think about making change, but you go back and forth," she says. "Change is a cyclical process that requires movement through progressive stages to learn new skills, from contemplating a change, to practicing it, to living life in a way that maintains it. Learning to live their lives 180 degrees different is a really big change. It can take a long time."

Regardless of the factors at play, "when children survive traumas, they inevitably blame themselves," she says. Shedding the guilt and shame are prerequisites to healing.

In one of his poems, Jesse-Ray addressed the death of his grandmother—the woman he called Mom—who had died in his arms as a young preteen.

"Because of that incident, he may feel that he's not worth love and attention," Clark says. "I've seen this in young people who've been through trauma. They get this close to a healthier lifestyle. Then it all goes to hell in a handbasket."

So will Jesse-Ray bounce from situation to situation, spiraling ever downward?

"Not necessarily," she says. "Through intensive counseling, he could root these things out and come to understand that it's not his fault. Such understanding is integral to recovery."

As for counselors and mentors who work with young people, she insists that the best approach is optimism and unwavering commitment:

"We don't know what their final chapters are going to be. We may never know what happens. But we can plant that seed. You can look at relapse as part of the process. Maybe, someday, something will click in a way that hasn't happened before. Some of them really do turn their lives around."

The primary goal for a person who is struggling is to work on the negative voice in his or her head. The negative voice carries a relentless message: You are worthless. You are unlovable.

According to Clark, this programming can be reversed, and the messages can be countered. "You have to believe that you are lovable even if you had people in your life who were supposed to love you and didn't."

Epilogue

At the end of August 2017, more than a month after our tenant had left our safe house, Hal stopped by the Bluefield Union Mission to ask if anyone had seen Jesse-Ray. He found out that they'd spotted him once or twice in the past thirty days. The word was that the woman with whom he'd been living had dumped him. He was hungry. The mission staff gave him food and a night at the motel, the same motel he'd been thrown out of earlier. But when Jesse-Ray showed up there, the owner shooed him away, wanting nothing to do with him. Had Jesse-Ray returned to the mission, the staff would have found him temporary lodging elsewhere. But only later did they learn of the reception that the motel owner had given him, and they heard it from the motel owner, not from Jesse-Ray. Where he went after that, they didn't know.

In September, Jesse-Ray surfaced—virtually, at least—in two emails to me from a homeless shelter in Beckley, West Virginia, about forty-five minutes north of Bluefield. He described himself as "somewhat clean" in terms of drugs.

I checked the Internet and saw that Beckley's homeless shelter offered counseling as well as the services of caseworkers. Was Jesse-Ray seeking help and support in new quarters? Apparently not. He said he'd hooked up with a "homie," didn't know how long he'd be saying, and implied he would soon depart. The shelter was just the latest waypoint in a transient life.

He added a note of thanks for Hal, whom he credited with motivating him to leave drug dealing behind.

"Tell Hal thanks for being there. It meant a lot to me. He is the reason why I left that life again. I went back to it and I just couldn't do it. Love y'all."

Months later, in January 2018, Jesse-Ray sent me another email, saying he'd moved back to his father's place in Virginia. Three days after he moved in, his father was taken to jail. Jesse-Ray didn't say why, only that "I hate being here." He claimed to have been clean and sober for three months and that he was trying to "stay away from Rick and them." He wrote that suicidal thoughts encased him "like an iron maiden." He asked to meet with me and Hal. I sent back an encouraging reply, asking that he call Hal or email me again so we would know where to find him. No reply came.

Bibliography

Preface

Lewis, J.-R. *Hillbilly Drug Baby: The Poems*. Christiansburg, Virginia: WriteLife Publishing, 2018.

Chapter 1

Centers for Disease Control and Prevention. "Infant and Maternal Characteristics in Neonatal Abstinence Syndrome—Selected Hospitals in Florida, 2010–2011." March 2015.

Centers for Disease Control and Prevention. "The Problem of Neonatal Abstinence Syndrome." August 2016.

Golden, J. L. *Message in a Bottle: The Making of Fetal Alcohol Syndrome*. Cambridge, Massachusetts: Harvard University Press, 2006.

Holloway, K. "The Massive Discrepancies Between Media Coverage of Mythical Crack Babies and Opiate-Dependent Babies." *AlterNet.org*, January 12, 2016.

Miller, A., and M. Warren. "Hospital-Based Surveillance for Neonatal Abstinence Syndrome in Tennessee." Tennessee Department of Health, Division of Family Health and Wellness, 2013. https://www.tn.gov/content/dam/tn/health/documents/nas/NAS_Annual_report _2013_FINAL.pdf

Oei, J.L., E. Melhuish, H. Uebel, N. Azzam, C. Breen, L. Burns, L. Hilder, et al. "Neonatal Abstinence Syndrome and High School Performance." *Pediatrics* 139, no. 2, February 2017.

Tennessee Commission on Children and Youth, Kids Count. "The State of the Child in Tennessee 2016." https://www.tn.gov/content/tn/tccy/kc/tccy-kcsoc16.html

Thomson-DeVeaux, A. "The New Moral Panic Over Drug-Dependent Babies." *American Prospect*, May 7, 2014.

Winerip, M. "Revisiting the 'Crack Babies' Epidemic That Was Not." *New York Times*, May 20, 2013.

Chapter 2

Centers for Disease Control and Prevention, "National Intimate Partner and Sexual Violence Survey – Summary Report." 2010. https://www.cdc.gov/violenceprevention/pdf/nisvs_report2010-a.pdf

McKinnon, M. "Perpetrators of Child Sexual Abuse Are Often Related to the Victim." The Lamplighter Movement, October 23, 2016.

Moore, D. A. "Domestic Violence in Appalachia with a Focus on Cabell County, West Virginia." MA thesis, Marshall University, 2004. http://citeseerx.ist.psu.edu/viewdoc/download?doi=10.1.1.94.7623&rep=rep1&type=pdf

U.S. Department of Health and Human Services, "Child Maltreatment 2014."

Chapter 3

Dotson-Lewis, B. L. "Speak Your Piece: Diane Sawyer in Eastern Kentucky." *The Daily Yonder*, February 15, 2009.

FAHE. "Appalachian Poverty." Accessed March 11, 2018. http://fahe.org/appalachian-poverty

Greenberg, P. "Disproportionality and Resource-Based Environmental Inequality: An Analysis of Neighborhood Proximity to Coal Impoundments in Appalachia." *Rural Sociology* 82, no. 1, August 2016: 149–178.

Hampson, R. "When W.Va. lost its voice: JFK's death still resonates." *USA Today*, October 27, 2013.

Janzer, C. "Could Outdoor Tourism Keep Millennials in Appalachia?" *Rewire.News*, September 8, 2017.

Rader, B. "I was born in poverty in Appalachia. 'Hillbilly Elegy' doesn't speak for me." *Washington Post*, September 1, 2017.

Rodd, S. "This Is What Poverty Looks Like." *Think Progress*, March 11, 2015.

Chapter 4

National Council for Juvenile and Family Court Judges. "NCJFCJ Resolves to Address Homeless Youth and Families." Accessed March 11, 2018. http://www.ncjfcj.org/Homeless-Youth-Resolution

Pokempner, J. "NCJFCJ Resolution Commits the Judiciary to Play a Pivotal Role in Seeing and Addressing the Risk of Homelessness That So Many Court Involved Youth Face," Juvenile Law Center, August 11, 2017.

US Interagency Council on Homelessness. "Federal Framework to End Youth Homelessness." Accessed March 11, 2018. https://www.usich.gov/tools-for-action/framework-for-ending-youth-homelessness

Chapter 5

AlcoholRehab.com. "Addiction and Emotional Immaturity." Accessed March 11, 2018. http://alcoholrehab.com/addiction-recovery/addiction-and-emotional-immaturity/

Brous, K. "Substance Abuse or Survival?" Foundation for Excellence in Mental Health Care, November 22, 2013.

Centers for Disease Control and Prevention. "About the CDC-Kaiser ACE Study." Accessed March 11, 2018. https://www.cdc.gov/violenceprevention/acestudy/about.html

Grimes, W. "Alice Miller, Psychoanalyst, Dies at 87. Laid Human Problems to Parental Acts." *New York Times*, April 26, 2010.

Inside the Alcoholic Brain. "Is Addiction an Attachment Disorder?" Accessed March 11, 2018. https://insidethealcoholicbrain.com/2014/11/28/is-addiction-an-attachment-disorder/

Lebron, A. M. *A Handbook for the Treatment of Alcoholism/Addiction, Family Involvement and Recovery*. Pittsburgh: Dorrance Publishing, 2014.

Chapter 6

Big Brothers Big Sisters of America. "Our Impact on Juvenile Justice." Accessed March 11, 2018. http://www.bbbs.org/impact-juvenile-justice/.

Cox, R. *The Spirit of Mentoring: A Manual for Adult Volunteers*. Auckland, New Zealand: Essential Resources, 2005.

Marks, L. "Mentoring Boys to Men." *Spirit of Change Magazine*, February 23, 2012.

Phillips-Jones, L., J. A. Walth, and C. Walth. "100 Ideas to Use When Mentoring Youth." The Mentoring Group. Accessed March 11, 2018. https://www.millersville.edu/mmap/files/ Curriculum/100%20Ideas%20to%20Use%20when%20Mentoring%20Youth.pdf

Chapter 7

Appalachian Magazine. "Say it Right! Appa-LAY-shuh = Nails on a Chalkboard!" January 4, 2017. Accessed March 11, 2018. http://appalachianmagazine.com/2017/01/04/say-it-right-appa-lay-shuh-nails-on-a-chalkboard/

Lilly, J., and R. Todd. "Inside Appalachia: Do We Talk Funny?" West Virginia Public Radio, June 12, 2015.

Mask, D. "Where the Streets Have No Name." *The Atlantic*, January/February 2013.

McCoy-Hall, T. "Is There a Correct Way to Pronounce 'Appalachia'?" *Odyssey*, September 8, 2013.

Puckett, A. "On the Pronunciation of Appalachia." *Now and Then: The Appalachian Magazine,* Summer 2000.

University of South Carolina, College of Arts and Sciences. "How Do You Pronounce Appalachia?" Accessed March 11, 2018. http://artsandsciences.sc.edu/appalachian english/node/790

Vorhees, B. "How Do You Say 'Appalachia'?" West Virginia Public Radio, November 6, 2015.

Chapter 8

Alm, D. "'Heroin(e)' Follows Three Women Fighting West Virginia's Opioid Epidemic." *Forbes*, September 14, 2017.

Corchado, A. "As Mexico's Drug Cartels Fracture, Violence and Travel Warnings Soar." *Dallas News*, August 25, 2017.

Executive Office of the President, Office of National Drug Control Policy. "Drug Trafficking Across the Southwest Border and Oversight of U.S. Counterdrug Assistance to Mexico." Statement before Congress by Michael P. Botticelli, November 17, 2015. Accessed March 11, 2018. https://obamawhitehouse.archives. gov/sites/default/files/ondcp/OLA/ ondcp_statement_for_nov_17_ senate_drug_caucus_mexico_hearing_--_final.pdf.

Gillman, O. "The United States of El Chapo: DEA cartel map of America shows that the fugitive drug lord dominates almost the whole of the US." *Daily Mail*, November 30, 2015.

Longmire, S. "Drug Cartels in U.S. as Big a Threat as Terrorism." CNN, December 9, 2010.

Matthews, D. "Here's What 'Breaking Bad' Gets Right, and Wrong, about the Meth Business." *Washington Post*, August 15, 2013.

Trejos, N. "USA Issues Travel Warning for Mexican Resort Town." *USA Today*, March 8, 2018.

Chapter 9

Foster Care to Success. "Foster Care: The Basics." Accessed March 11, 2018. http://www.fc2success.org/knowledge-center/foster-care-the-basics/

Garcia, Antonio. "To Counter Child Abuse, Administrators and Case Workers Need Support to Implement Evidence-Based Improvements." *Social Work Helper*, August 27, 2017.

Chapter 10

Courtney, M. E., A. Dworsky, and C. Smithgall. "Supporting Youth Transitioning out of Foster Care." Issue Brief 1: Educational Programs, Urban Institute, December 2014. https://www.urban.org/sites/default/files/publication/43266/2000127-Supporting-Youth-Transitioning-out-of-Foster-Care.pdf

Foster Care to Success. "Challenges and Solutions." Accessed March 11, 2018. http://www.fc2success.org/knowledge-center/challenges-solutions/#solutions

Legal Center for Foster Care and Education. "National Factsheet on the Educational Outcomes of Children in Foster Care," January 2014.

US Department of Health and Human Services, "Child Maltreatment 2014."

Chapter 11

Brand, R. Interview by Bill Maher. *Real Time with Bill Maher*, HBO, Oct. 6, 2017. Audio available on YouTube, 4:06, https://youtu.be/8NaJdHZSPqM

Howard, J. "Religious Thoughts Trigger Reward Systems Like Love, Drugs." CNN, November 29, 2016.

Lavitt, J. "Inside Addiction Treatment with Dr. Marvin Seppala." *The Fix*, May 15, 2015.

Liotta, J. "Does Science Show What 12 Steps Know?" *National Geographic*, August 10, 2013.

McPeake, J. D. "William James, Bill Wilson, and the development of Alcoholics Anonymous (A.A.)." Accessed March 11, 2018. The Dublin Group Inc. http://dubgrp.com/content/ william-james-bill-wilson-and-development-alcoholics-anonymous-aa

NPR. "For Addicts, There May Be Another Road to Wellness," June 8, 2014. Accessed March 11, 2018. https://www.npr.org/2014/06/08/319527437/for-addiction-the-road-to-wellness-has-more-than-one-path

Chapter 12

Arizona State University Now. "Education Student Takes the Path Less Traveled." January 17, 2014. Accessed March 11, 2018. https://asunow.asu.edu/content/education-student-takes-path-less-traveled

Faller, M. B. "'Sparky Slam' Will Create Supportive Space for Teens to Share Poetry." *Arizona State University Now*, March 23, 2017.

Goshay, C. "Canton Christian Rap Concert Aims to Spread Message." *Canton Repository*, September 2, 2017.

Hernandez, V. "Sevin Has Grand Plan to Bring Gospel to America's Hoods." *Rapzilla*, May 5, 2015.

Jocson, K. M. *Youth Poets: Empowering Literacies in and Out of Schools*. New York City: Peter Lang Inc., 2008.

Mahiri, J., and S. Sablo. "Writing for Their Lives: The Non-School Literacy of California's Urban African American Youth." *Journal of Negro Education* 65, no. 2, (Spring 1996): 164–80.

Williams, W. "Listen to the Poet: What Schools Can Learn from a Diverse Spoken Word." PhD diss., Arizona State University, 2015.

Chapter 13

Garcia, A. "To Counter Child Abuse, Administrators and Case Workers Need Support to Implement Evidence-Based Improvements." *Social Work Helper*, August 27, 2017.

Kelly, J. "Child Welfare Ideas from the Experts #11." *The Chronicle of Social Change*, August 3, 2017.

Pokempner, J. "Making a Truly Healthy Transition to Adulthood Relies on a Strong Medicaid Program and Our Commitment to Enhance Access to Quality Care." Juvenile Law Center Blog, August 4, 2017.

Chapter 14

Baird, S. "Stereotypes of Appalachia Obscure a Diverse Picture." NPR, April 6, 2014.

Bowling Green State University Libraries. "Hillbilly Elegy: Interviews with the Author." The resource guide for the 2017-18 Common Experience book selection, J.D. Vance's *Hillbilly Elegy*. Accessed March 11, 2018. http://libguides.bgsu.edu/c.php?g=671519&p=4728589.

Eubanks, Katie. "Surviving Southern Stereotypes at the Movies." *Clarion-Ledger*, September 29, 2017.

Jones, S. "J.D. Vance, the False Prophet of Blue America." *New Republic*, November 17, 2016.

Phillips, R. "40 Years Later, 'Deliverance' Still Draws Tourists, Stereotypes." CNN, June 22, 2012.

Rosenblum, C. "Hillbillies who code: the former miners out to put Kentucky on the tech map." *The Guardian*, April 21, 2017.

Shaffer, A. "The 'H' word: fighting negative language stereotypes in Appalachia." Eberly College of Arts and Sciences, West Virginia University, June 12, 2017.

Chapter 15

B., Hamilton. *Twelve-Step Sponsorship: How It Works*. Center City, Minnesota: Hazelden Publishing, 1996.

ElevationsHealth.com. "Tough Love: Letting Your Addict Hit Rock Bottom." June 9, 2016. https://elevationshealth.com/tough-love-letting-your-addict-hit-rock-bottom/

Jay, D. *No More Letting Go: The Spirituality of Taking Action Against Alcoholism and Drug Addiction*. New York City: Bantam Dell, 2006.

National Institute on Drug Abuse. "What to Do If Your Adult Friend or Loved One Has a Problem with Drugs." Accessed March 11, 2018. https://www.drugabuse.gov/related-topics/treatment/what-to-do-if-your-adult-friend-or-loved-one-has-problem-drugs

Singal, J. "The Tragic, Pseudoscientific Practice of Forcing Addicts to 'Hit Rock Bottom.'" *New York Magazine*, May 2016.

Szalavitz, M. "Why Addiction Is a Learning Disorder." Interview by Gabrielle Glaser, *Daily Beast*, April 8, 2016.

Chapter 16

Clark, F. B. Interview by Andrea Brunais, September 2017.

About the Author

Award-winning journalist and author Andrea Brunais spent 30 years as an editor, reporter, and columnist for Media General, Creative Loafing, and Knight Ridder newspapers. A freelance writer and author of both fiction and nonfiction, she has won awards including Silver medalist, fiction, in the Florida Authors and Publishers Association nationwide contest, 2015.

Her freelance work has appeared in outlets such as the *Christian Science Monitor, TravelPulse.com, DuPont Registry,* and *Appalachian Voice.* Her newspaper honors include first place in Commentary from the Florida Press Club, a Robert Kennedy Journalism Award, and first place in the annual Southern Newspaper Publishers competition.

She works in higher-education communications and is the creator and executive producer of the web-episode series Save Our Towns.

For more about Brunais and *Hillbilly Drug Baby: The Story,* please visit www.hillbillydrugbaby.com